MW01030995

THE

ADVENTURE

BEGINS WHEN THE PLAN

FALLS APART

THE ADVENTURE

BEGINS WHEN THE PLAN

FALLS APART

CONVERT A CRISIS INTO COMPANY SUCCESS

JIM BAKER

Published by Advantage, Charleston, South Carolina.
Member of Advantage Media Group.

ADVANTAGE is a registered trademark, and the Advantage colophon is a trademark of Advantage Media Group, Inc.

Printed in the United States of America.

10 9 8 7 6 5 4 3 2 1

ISBN: 978-1-59932-855-3
LCCN: 2017942328

Cover design and layout by Katie Biondo.

This publication is designed to provide accurate and authoritative information in regard to the subject matter covered. It is sold with the understanding that the publisher is not engaged in rendering legal, accounting, or other professional services. If legal advice or other expert assistance is required, the services of a competent professional person should be sought.

Advantage Media Group is proud to be a part of the Tree Neutral® program. Tree Neutral offsets the number of trees consumed in the production and printing of this book by taking proactive steps such as planting trees in direct proportion to the number of trees used to print books. To learn more about Tree Neutral, please visit **www.treeneutral.com.**

Advantage Media Group is a publisher of business, self-improvement, and professional development books. We help entrepreneurs, business leaders, and professionals share their Stories, Passion, and Knowledge to help others Learn & Grow. Do you have a manuscript or book idea that you would like us to consider for publishing? Please visit advantagefamily.com or call **1.866.775.1696.**

TABLE OF CONTENTS

A WORD FROM THE AUTHOR

Before I begin, I would like to thank my wife, Colleen; my children; my siblings, especially my brother Mike; my in-laws; and of course, my mother. Without them in my life, supporting and believing in me, I would not have been able to write this book.

As you can see I am a very lucky person. I have a great family, I am healthy, and I had a great ride from the start to the selling of my business. I believe most people could do what I did. It didn't require significant intelligence, a huge amount of money, or any extraordinary skill set. I, and those I partnered with along the way, happened to be in the right place at the right time to experience setbacks and successes. We had hard-working, loyal, and caring people work for us. I have also been fortunate to have mentors and advisors who helped me all along the way. Today, through my consulting firm, Sumus, I aim to serve as a mentor in turn, guiding entrepreneurs and business owners toward success by helping them build the value of their businesses, with the goal that they will eventually be able to exit the business lucratively.

I have been in business for thirty years now, and I have grown accustomed to giving my unvarnished opinion. In consulting, I often have to give direct, frank advice on what works and what doesn't, where a business is going, and where it is going *wrong*. I enjoy the work I do, though I confess that I ask business owners to engage in some difficult self-reflection and self-criticism.

I don't do this because I think I'm a hotshot or the smartest guy in the room. Quite the opposite; as I explain in chapter 1, I see myself as a fairly ordinary guy, a husband and father of four, who has learned from his own experiences of screwing up, going astray, and running into obstacles face first. Through the connections I have made in business, and even more so through my consulting, I have also had the privilege of observing other people and how they react to difficult situations, whether the outcome is positive or negative.

I have developed a knack for spotting problems, and my style is to point them out so that people can start to go about fixing them. Whenever I focus on the negative in what follows, it is always with the aim of directing business owners away from those types of outcomes and toward the success that I am confident every business can have. I tell a lot of stories here, hopefully in a way that you will find entertaining, but also with the aim of presenting possibilities that you may be able to relate to your own situation and that you can learn from going forward.

To that end, I share my stories as directly and authentically as possible. That means asking you, as the reader, to engage in some tough self-reflection sometimes too. This task makes some people uncomfortable, but I know from experience that you will come out on the other end of it having learned some valuable lessons. At the end of the day, business and life are both all about the experiences we have and how we deal with them, and I hope this book provides some valuable guidance for this going forward.

CHAPTER 1

A RIDE IN THE COUNTRY

"The adventure begins when the plan falls apart." These were my son's words. They struck me as very insightful; they also helped me turn my day around.

His words immediately before that had been, "Hey Dad, I think the back tire has a leak." At that, I threw the tire iron on the ground in frustration and disgust. I had been holding the tire iron because I was already replacing a flat *front* tire. That was annoying, but at least we had a spare and could continue our journey. Now, on the other hand—we were going to end up with two flats, and we had only one spare. This was *definitely* not the way this day was supposed to play out.

After all, it was a beautiful, unseasonably warm Tuesday morning in Ireland. I had been traveling with my son Daniel from Lahinch to Ballybunion, about an hour-and-a-half drive, with the Atlantic Ocean sparkling on the horizon, on a week-long golf trip to celebrate my son's college graduation. I had driven in Ireland before, but I was a little nervous that day. The rental company had given me an Audi A4, which is a good bit bulkier (and higher-end) than the Ford Focus I had expected, and the country roads we were driving were quite narrow. I was nervous mainly about encountering oncoming traffic; but I was still enjoying the beautiful day and the time I was spending with my son.

Then, of course, it happened: I encountered oncoming traffic in the form of an eighteen-wheeler—which was quite intimidating on those narrow roads. I moved to the left to give the driver plenty of room, and I heard—and felt—the stone wall along that side of the road as the car scraped nastily up against it. I kicked myself for damaging the rental car, but I reminded myself that I had insurance, and it would all be fine. Of course, just a little way down the road, I heard—and felt—the thump, thump, thump of a flat tire

Now I was really mad at myself for my carelessness. I pulled over in front of what looked like a church, but it seemed to be abandoned. Next to it was a barn occupied only by dogs and cows. The dogs came to investigate, and one took the liberty of "marking" the flat tire as his territory, in case I was starting to feel too sunny about the situation. Of course, there was nothing to do but replace the tire, so I got the spare and tools from the trunk and started jacking up the car.

It was just at that point that my son, who had been giving me a hand with the tools but had otherwise been pretty quiet up to this point, spoke up to tell me that the back tire seemed to be leaking air as well. I checked, and sure enough, air was escaping from it and it was quickly going flat. My anger with myself at this point boiled over and merged with a sense of panic, even of hopelessness: we were stuck. I apologized to my son—I felt like my actions had derailed our whole agenda for the day, and he wouldn't get to experience this beautiful golf course. The trip, the way I saw it, wasn't going to be as perfect as

I had imagined. That's when he responded, "Hey, Dad, don't worry about it. When the plan falls apart, the adventure begins."

Like I said, I was struck by his words, and I decided he was exactly right. I could sit in the dirt and wait for someone to come help me, ensuring that my son and I would miss our tee-time; or I could take action. My son's mature insight had bolstered my confidence that this situation could be remedied. I had an international cell phone, so I called the car rental agency. They wouldn't be able to come get the car for two hours. We walked down the road to a nearby house, where we found a kind family that helped us by offering to wait with the car for the rental company and arranging a ride to a nearby ferry, which would take us to within fifteen minutes of our destination.

After a few more phone calls, we were able to relax and enjoy the trip; the rest of the week was thankfully uneventful. It gave me some time to reflect; that's when I started thinking about the ideas in this book.

I was on the ferry when I first had the idea for a book. I had gone outside for some air and was looking out over the water, and my son's words were stuck in my head. Having been in business for almost thirty years, I have a habit of applying a lot of the concepts I come across to the business world, and this was no exception. All of us who have been in business can recall times when our plans fell apart in our hands. What happened next was up to us. We end up in a predicament, and we have basically two choices. On one side, we can sit around feeling guilty about bad decisions we have made; we can blame others (employees, the market, global events, or the rich), or we can deny the reality of the situation. In other words, we can *avoid* tackling the problem head-on.

On the other side, we can see the predicament as an opportunity to take action and strike off in a new direction. I have come to think this decision plays the central role in determining whether a business owner is successful or unsuccessful.

MY CAREER SO FAR

I have learned this lesson, along with many others, the hard way. I owned and ran a business for twenty-seven years, at the end of which I was able to sell my company for enough money that I would be able to do what I wanted with my life. I saw myself as successful; in the process, though, I got lucky—many times. I realized that I had been through many occasions of plans going awry and leading to adventures, which weren't fun at the time but that I learned a great deal from. Also, I didn't do it by myself; I had mentors, advisors, and great employees who helped me every step of the way. My experiences and the support I received from others made my business stronger, and I became a better leader over time due to adversity.

My career essentially started with Atlantic Search Group, an IT search firm owned by my father and his business partner. I started there in 1987, and, by way of stories I'll tell in chapters 2 and 3, became a co-owner and then sole owner of the business within a few years. When I first became a business owner, I was young and hadn't had a lot of business mentorship, so I did a lot of learning as I went along.

The business soon migrated from a search focus to a staffing focus, and I aspired to take the company national, so the name no longer made sense and we rebranded as simply ASG. We continued to grow, and by the early 2000s we were mainly staffing data professionals and biostatisticians for clinical research trials for pharmaceutical firms. This sector took a hit at that time, though, because pharmaceutical companies were going through a major cost-cutting process; our gross margins dropped from 35 percent down to about 18 or 19 percent in the space of a year.

This forced the ASG team to reflect, and we decided to keep our researchers in-house and let the pharmaceutical companies hire us to do the clinical trials for them. As a result, we changed our staffing arm to focus on functional outsourcing, and we also moved into the world of contract research (CRO) work by acquiring an already-existing CRO named Ockham, using their existing work as a foundation moving forward. About 80 percent of the work that company was doing was in oncology. At that point, in 2009, we did another rebranding, at which point we changed our name to Ockham and sharpened our focus on oncology clinical trials.

Over the course of the next five years, the company grew considerably, including the acquisition of a Scottish oncology CRO called Nexus Oncology in January 2012. This allowed us to greatly expand the reach of the company and increase profitability. As a result, between the time ASG became Ockham and the time we sold Ockham four and a half years later, the company's value had more than quadrupled.

In sum, the business I owned began as a local search firm and over the next twenty-seven years transformed into a global CRO providing clinical trial services to biotech and pharmaceutical companies. In the meantime, we grew organically, tried and failed with new business units, acquired two new companies, expanded, and contracted. I tell the stories of some of these developments in the following chapters. The sale of Ockham in 2014 to Chiltern International in July 2014 exceeded my expectations; I was fortunate, able to achieve something I had been dreaming of for years.

None of it was easy; bad things happened all along the way that forced me to step back, adjust, and tackle the situation in a new way. Plans fell apart, and new adventures began. That's business; that's life. That's also the idea behind all of the stories I tell in this book.

Since selling Ockham, I have been able to start a consulting and advising firm, Sumus, where I draw on my own hard-learned lessons and hands-on experience as a CEO to help entrepreneurs and business owners build the value of their own companies. I consult with other businesses, see their struggles and pain points, and learn from them as well. I now want to share those lessons in this book; just as I learned from my mentors, I now hope business leaders and entrepreneurs can learn from me.

WHAT DO I HAVE TO OFFER

Why listen to me? Am I just another CEO with some hotshot idea that I think will help you get rich quick?

Not at all; I think one of the reasons I can help people who own businesses is just that I'm so much like them. I'm really a pretty ordinary person. My father wasn't a senator or a millionaire but a hard-working middle-class guy; he provided for the family well, so I don't have any stories of terrible suffering from my childhood. Like I said, I was young and inexperienced when I started. I didn't achieve success overnight. I worked hard, had long days at the office, and did the daily grind of courting customers on the phone all day long.

My parents didn't pamper me. I faced rejection and failure at a number of points when I was young. I think that these experiences have actually helped me move on when something bad happens. This is a key business skill because rejection happens all the time in business—from the client, the employee, the market, whatever. The key is understanding the messages that you are getting—listening to your clients, your employees, and the market. Finding and listening to mentors and advisors is also essential. This kind of listening is what makes a great business leader and will help you navigate some of the crazy obstacles you will surely encounter in owning a business.

If I can be as successful as I have been, other ordinary folks like me can be too. Anyone who finds himself or herself in the position of having the opportunity to open or run a business at some point in time can be successful. All you have to do is learn from your mistakes, have the discipline to make tough decisions, and meet challenges with confidence and determination rather than despair.

This is, of course, easier said than done. In the pages that follow I discuss key mistakes that many business owners make. Some of these can be crippling to a business, especially if the owner does not quickly own up to the mistake and take steps to right the ship. This, I think, is the key to success: recognizing when things are not going as planned and being willing to change course. My hope now is that you will read and understand what I have to say and apply it to your own situation.

What I really want is for this book to speak to business owners, to help me be a mentor to them, and to get them to think about their purpose—why did they get into business in the first place, and what are their hopes and expectations for their businesses in the future? This leads us to the important theme of the exit strategy, which will be recurring throughout the book. The fact of the matter is, if you are a business owner, then at some point you will *stop* being a business owner—no ifs, ands, or buts about it. Every business owner exits in some way or another. It often happens a lot sooner than you think—whether that is a positive or a negative thing. You have to be adaptable and prepared.

HEADING FOR THE EXIT

Think of it this way: most likely, if you own a house, at some point down the road it is going to be sold, and it is in your interest to arrange for the most profitable sale possible. As a result, you have to maintain and update the house as the years go by. If you don't, you (or your heirs) will suffer in the marketplace. Even if that house means the world to you and you love it with all of its flaws, the market is not going to see it that way. If you take your subjective valuation of the house to the market as your expected sale price, you are bound for disappointment.

Businesses are just like houses in that respect. How you value your business and why you started it are all great starting points for getting your business going, but that won't ensure you a successful future exit, because your business will change as the market changes; nothing stays the same for long in the business world, and if your business doesn't keep up, then your exit will not be as successful as you hoped for at the start. You have to always be aware of what the market, and your clients or customers, are telling you about the value of your business, and don't get caught up in illusions about what your business is worth that don't align with that.

If you have a full understanding of what your business's value is, and where that value comes from, you can succeed. If, on top of that, you can achieve employee engagement through a clear sense of *mission*, maintain a clean set of books, and produce high-quality work—then that's it, you have won! You have secured future employment for your employees, whether with yourself or with a new company; you have made it possible to cash out, if that's one of your goals; and you have left yourself the option of doing something else in your future.

In this book, I discuss some situations I have encountered that come to mind when I think of my little Ireland adventure. These are stories, my own and those of other people, of the unexpected happening—in a bad way, in other words, plans falling apart. In the positive cases, the person whose plans fell apart grasped the opportunity to change for the better and to learn; those that did not, did not do so well. The lesson is that, if you embrace the notion that "when the plan goes awry the adventure begins," you will more likely assure for yourself a successful exit from business or from your working life.

CHAPTER 2

UNTIMELY EXIT

It was a cold, January day in 1988 when my father called me into his office. As soon as he spoke I realized that this wasn't going to be a typical meeting. He told me that he had been having trouble breathing when he tried to sleep, so he had gone to the doctor, who had found a "spot" on his lung. He would have to have surgery and be out for a week. All I could think of was Johnny Bench, the Hall of Fame catcher for the Cincinnati Reds in the mid 1970s, who also had a spot on his lung and was treated and lived to be a great baseball player. My fathered downplayed the concern, so I was confident that he would be able to fight through it.

When I talked to my mother later that day, though, she told me the doctor had found a grapefruit-sized tumor on his left lung. So much for a spot. After a couple of trips in and out of the hospital, we discovered that the cancer had spread to his brain; he passed away just weeks later.

This wasn't the plan.

At the time, I had been working for about a year at one of the two companies my father owned with a business partner. A couple of years before that, he and his partner had incorporated Atlantic Search Group (ASG), an information technology (IT) staffing company. However, the other business kept getting all of their attention, and ASG had been dormant since its incorporation.

Basically, he had explained to me, they wanted to recruit and place programmers, and if I were to come on board, he would give me a desk and a phone—desktops were not commonplace yet. I would work for 100 percent commission, getting paid on the basis of how many placements I made. When I made a placement I would get 50 percent, and the company would get the other half. I detected potential here for getting my career started—and for making more money, as I had previously been on a fixed salary with limited potential for advancement. With a business that was basically a start-up, the possibilities were much more open, and I was excited at the prospect. So I took the desk and got to work.

The first year went well. I was basically left alone—there was only a small handful of employees and no management apart from my father—and I had already doubled my income. At the pace I was working, I quickly became the lead revenue generator in the company. I sensed that I was a large part of the growth of the company, so I became excited at the possibilities for doing great things in and with this company. Also, according to my father's plan, I would be taking over control of the company when he retired a few years down the road.

After struggling through the emotional difficulty of the ordeal of losing my father, I went back to work and was left thinking about my future again. This had *definitely not* been the plan.

SO WHAT IS PLAN B?

The plan, as both my father and I had understood it, was that he would work for about five more years, get the company on a solid footing, and then retire with a steady income stream, at which point I would take over the business and work on growing it. But this was just the problem: the company was definitely *not* on a solid footing at the time, and we had never really talked in any detail about how his exit and my succession to leadership of the company would take place. Not to mention we didn't have a back-up plan in case of unexpected catastrophic events—like his death.

His death threw the company into disarray. Plan A (which itself was not very well thought out) had fallen apart, and Plan B was nowhere to be found. Furthermore, Martin, my father's business partner, owned 50 percent of the company but had been completely uninvolved in the running of the company up to that point. The other 50 percent owner now was my mother, who, of course, was still reeling from my father's death and was not a businessperson.

These chaotic situations, brought about by unexpected events that disrupt the ownership structure, can develop quickly when the owners have not put a plan in place to deal with this. In fairness, people who are starting a business typically do not have succession or exit plans on their minds. Unfortunately, life happens in business, and if a rough plan is not in place, then things can get chaotic. I was faced with this, perhaps somewhat ironically, at the very beginning of my career rather than the end, and in my advisory business I have seen these types of situations play themselves out many times. The lesson is plain: companies whose leaders take the time to draw up detailed disaster recovery or succession plans, including what to do in case of the loss of an owner, are more likely to survive such upheavals;

those that do not take that time are going to struggle through them. Yes, this involves a bit of expecting the unexpected, but a Plan B for a company's ownership structure is absolutely crucial .

Honestly, my first thought was, "Do I really want to continue with this thing or should I just go get a job someplace else?" After a couple weeks, though, things had settled down a little and I was thinking clearly. I knew that I wanted to continue growing this business that I had helped my father get up and running. That had sort of been the plan after all, right? My father, while 50 percent owner, had been 100 percent leader of the company; I had contributed significantly to the success of the company in that first year; and I thought I could really grow the company and go places with it. Given my contribution to the (at the time, little) value of the business, I thought I could basically buy my father's business partner out through sweat equity.

Plan B for a company's ownership structure is absolutely crucial.

So my adventure began. I had a *new* plan—a new plan that my father's partner promptly dismissed. It quickly became evident to me that Martin did not have much respect for me as a twenty-four-year-old professional; he had more respect for, and a better relationship with, my more experienced thirty-eight-year-old colleague Peter. But I was bringing in most of the revenue, so it didn't make sense to get rid of me. He decided to try to bind my colleague and me in with a little bit of equity in the company—6 percent for me, 18 percent for Peter, over the next three years. He also proposed eventually making Peter the CEO.

This was galling to me and unacceptable. Martin had been absent up to the point of my father's death, and, as I was the primary revenue generator in the business, I thought I should be the one to run it and own it. Due to my performance, I naturally thought of myself as the leader of the company and thought I deserved considerably more equity—sweat equity.

AGAINST SWEAT EQUITY

This was the second lesson I was about to learn: I was naïve. I didn't understand much about the way the business world works. I had no experience with the responsibilities of hiring and firing; I was just working nine- or ten-hour days on the phone. Just because the other employees weren't doing that, and thus not bringing in as much revenue, doesn't mean they were lazy; they were just in different situations. In fact, looking back on it, I now realize that Peter probably felt the same way I did. As the senior member of the company, with more experience, certainly he should be in charge, right?

That's not necessarily right either, of course—but these kinds of assumptions are all too common in the business world. Martin was on the right track in realizing that the person that is generating your sales is not necessarily your most valuable employee. Getting a raise every year is not the same as being entitled to an increase in your ownership share every year. These do not go hand-in-hand.

There is a lesson here for business owners as well. Some owners construct their exit plan around the notion that their key employees will gradually take ownership of the business through increasing equity shares. This provides for the owner's exit and—the idea is—helps with retention. On this model, these owners allow their employees to buy them out with the profits of the company. The owner is basically giving them ownership money to buy into the business. Although this is not my preferred option, it has worked for some. In addition, some allow for employees to earn sweat equity purely; they do not require those employees to go to the trouble of borrowing money to actually buy those equity shares.

But this is exactly what they *should* do. If they don't, then those employees end up not having skin in the game. I know very well that, in this day and age, when employees tend to stick around for only two or three years, there is a lot of pressure on business owners to figure out ways to keep their key employees vested in the business. There are good strategies for doing this, but rewarding performance or loyalty solely with equity is not one of them.

One of the best pieces of advice I ever received was: "Whatever you do, never give equity to anybody." My attorney said this to me early on, not long after my father passed away. "What do you mean?" I asked. "Make them pay for it. If they're not willing to write a check, to do the work to get the money to buy the stock, then they are not valuing their equity the way it should be valued. You don't want to be stuck down the road with a silent owner making money from the sweat off your back."

He was absolutely right. It is a mistake to try to retain employees by just offering them stock. Equity is the most valuable thing you can offer. If you have high performers or key employees, the reward for their performance will be reflected in their pay and any monetary bonuses and, of course, commissions they get. Equity goes above and beyond this and should not be given without an investment in exchange. If you just give it to people, they are less likely to really care for it; people will care for and value something more if they have to pay for it. It's human nature. In other words, would you give a portion of your house to someone? If you aren't willing to give your house away, you certainly shouldn't be willing to give your company away.

It is a mistake to try to retain employees by just offering them stock.

After just a few years as a consultant helping entrepreneurs grow and increase the value of their companies, I have seen a lot of these companies, especially young ones, that are afraid to lose their high performers, so they practically back the Brinks truck up for some of these top sales folks and give them a ton of money and some sweat equity. Some of these employees can basically hold the company hostage because the owner is afraid to not acquiesce to everything that individual wants. Then, when they do, 95 percent of the time it backfires: the person ends up not performing at that top level anymore; either they get lazy or they get promoted to some management or other leadership role when, quite frankly, they're not managers or leaders, they're salespeople. They are wired to sell, not manage, train, coach, and lead. They are valuable and, therefore, there are other ways to retain them. In some cases, the business has evolved into something else where that person just no longer fits.

In the end, the business owner is now stuck with someone who may be a great salesperson but is not good at other things that the owner needs them to do as the company grows and matures. A top performer is not always the most valuable employee, let alone the best leader.

So, thinking back to my situation starting out, Martin was both right and wrong. He was right in recognizing that my being the top performer didn't mean I should be the boss. But he was wrong in his strategy of granting Peter and me equity for sticking around.

A top performer is not always the most valuable employee, let alone the best leader.

He also didn't think enough about his own exit. He needed to ask himself, "Do I really still want to be responsible and liable for this business, or do I want to figure out some way for someone to buy me out of ASG so that I can maximize my buyout?" Here again, the lack of exit strategy was a big mistake. My recommendation for him now would have been to set a price, based on objective criteria, for purchase of the business and then find a buyer willing to pay that price. Once that was agreed to, he could then decide on how he wanted to be paid by the buyer.

Martin also failed to recognize that age and experience are no better indicators of leadership than high sales performance. In choosing employees for leadership roles, business owners have to take a look at the talent in their company, and if there is a thirty-year-old who displays leadership qualities more effectively than a fifty-year-old, then they should go with the thirty-year-old. In the case of Peter and me, Peter in fact didn't have much interest in building the business. He saw it as more of a lifestyle business. He just wanted to come to work day after day and take a paycheck home. I respect that, but my vision for the business was very different. I was motivated to really make a go of things with this business. I though that if I were in charge then I could make ASG a really good company; I was willing to devote myself to growing the company. I thought that made me ultimately more suited to being the leader of the company.

LOOK BEFORE YOU LEAP

Unsatisfied with the arrangement Martin had worked out, I decided to talk to Peter to see if he would be interested in a partnership. I ultimately offered to partner up with him 50/50 so that we could buy the business outright. He agreed. I borrowed a little money and paid my share, and there I was. At twenty-four years old, I was a young copresident of a company. I had thought that I deserved to be in charge, and then, once I ended up achieving what I wanted to achieve, I realized, "I don't know anything about running a business! I have to clean up these financials, I've got to do employee reviews, I've got to lead by example, and I don't know how to do *any* of those things!"

As I mentioned, the company as my father left it was a mess. The financial situation in particular was going to require expertise that I did not have. Though the company was generating revenue, it was financially noncompliant. My father and his business partner had come straight into business ownership from jobs in very large corporations where they had not had leadership responsibilities. As a result, they didn't have a sense for how urgently they needed an accountant and an attorney. My father had delayed on hiring an accountant, and as a result the books and the company's tax situation were a mess. Their time in the corporate world had not prepared them for business ownership as well as they had thought it would.

This type of situation is more common than you might think. As strange as it sounds, a lot of business owners don't really *plan* to be business owners. Many fall into it accidentally or due to a sudden opportunity that they can't pass up—which is basically what happened to me. Even those who have always dreamed of opening their own store, restaurant, whatever, don't really go into it thinking of themselves as *business owners*. When this realization occurs—when you're up against a responsibility and a set of decisions you didn't bargain for—that is when the adventure begins, just as it did for me.

If you hope to start a business, or even if there's a possibility that you will end up in an ownership position, be aware of the responsibilities and liabilities that are going to crop up for you in that situation. Look for mentors who have gone through what you are going through and who can warn you about, and help you navigate, obstacles. If you will be working with partners (which I'll be talking about more in the next chapter), make sure that there is a discussion about who is going to be doing what. Also, someone needs to be on top of the financial aspect of things—somebody has to do the books; you don't want to generate a lot of revenue and have to shut the company down because the books are a mess.

This is *almost* what happened to me—ASG could have been shut down if I had not immediately hired an accountant to take control of our finances. Then this story would have been over before it even started.

Not that taking control of ASG at the age of twenty-four had been my plan; it was the adventure that started once my original plan was derailed. I had quickly learned the hard way about the importance of having a succession plan, clear agreements about all aspects of ownership in general, and financial discipline. So there I was, in charge and without a definitive blueprint about what to do next. Was I ready for business ownership? Fortunately, I had a partner—though this had problems of its own.

CHAPTER 3

PARTNER TROUBLE

Her name was Madelyn. Peter, my partner, had hired Madelyn to work for him. She was the only person he had on his staff other than his sister, who worked for him only sporadically. On my side, I had a small team, just three people. Peter and I each had our own set of clients and our own staff, managing things pretty much independently.

Peter's smaller team was producing considerably less revenue, and business was starting to slow down for him. He decided he didn't want the added expense of keeping Madelyn on, so he let her go.

I wasn't thrilled about this—though she was on his staff, she was an employee of *our* company, and I, being in charge of payroll, was writing her paycheck every month. I thought I could use Madelyn on my team, but Peter fired her without consulting me. So, the next day, I invited her to lunch and asked if she wanted to join my team. She liked the company, so she was happy to come back on—as long as she worked for me rather than Peter. I should have been concerned about this at the time because it indicated further difficulties to come.

Now it was Peter's turn to not be thrilled. It got under his skin; looking back I don't think I handled the situation as well as I could have, but at the time I thought he had gone behind *my* back and made a mistake in firing a perfectly good employee. And now neither of us was thrilled with the other.

We were pulling in opposite directions, and this was not the first time. The fact is our partnership was immature. We didn't meet regularly, partly because we didn't feel the need to but also because he didn't think I had anything to offer, as a much younger colleague, and I wanted to avoid confronting him with some of the things that were bothering me. Our disagreement over Madelyn's place in the company, though, finally clued me in: the partnership wasn't working, and something had to give.

THE ALIGNMENT PROBLEM

Don't get me wrong, Peter and I generally got along as copresidents and owners of ASG for those first three years. We had a good working relationship, no conflicts were openly erupting in the workplace, and we were getting things done. The plan was working, in a way—we were both making a living. But it was not the way I envisioned it.

Peter and I had different strategic visions for the business. He saw it as a lifestyle business, while I had an entrepreneurial take on it; I wanted to build the company up, take it nationwide, and so forth. Also, we were at different points in our lives—in particular, he had kids and I didn't, which meant I was able to devote more time and attention to work. This also meant that my sales team was producing double the revenue his group was generating. The value of his equity was increasing due to the work of my team. I would be lying if I told you this wasn't gnawing at me daily.

Our partnership had been a marriage of convenience, with the goal of buying out Martin, the previous owner. We hadn't really talked much about sharing job responsibilities, and neither had we talked about general strategy: where we wanted to go with the business, what our visions for it were. Because of this, we ended up basically running two separate businesses out of the same office. Not only did we differ on strategy, but we also oversaw two different cultures. It was almost like *A Tale of Two Cities*. We weren't a united company.

I was trying to make this business a real business—keeping it as professional as possible. This was before the days of business casual, so I was wearing a suit to the office every day, for example. On Peter's side, things were quite different. Peter ran his side of the business the way he wanted to—namely, very casually, from his team's casual dress to the fact that his sister brought her dog in to the office every day (which drove me crazy). These things symbolize a difference in mind-set and vision for the business. All of this signaled to me that Peter's mind-set was, "Hey, it's my company, and I can do what I want."

These little things built tension, which was a problem, especially given our lack of communication. A business partner is someone you see day in and day out, sometimes more than your family. So it's a relationship both have to think about and work on. It's like a marriage in that respect, and if things are not going well, a lot of negativity emerges, which can spill over into your life. Even a marriage of convenience, like Peter's and mine, has to work out some agreements beforehand about goals and about culture. If Peter and I had spent time on this at the front end, when we were first talking about partnering, and had communicated frequently after that, then we could have avoided a lot of difficulties that we were now facing daily.

As I mentioned, every time there was an issue or a conflict, I would delay meeting with Peter as much as possible, simply because I knew it would be unpleasant. When a partnership is not working well over time, it becomes much more difficult to communicate with your partner. The less you communicate, the more separated you're going to become. So it's a vicious cycle that is harmful to you, to your employees, and to your business as a whole. That's why it is crucial to communicate early and often.

Fortunately, from the perspective of office culture, Peter and I had a very small staff, most of whom were on my team and aligned with that culture. But as a business gets bigger and bigger, much bigger problems will arise if the company does not have one set culture, one set of values, and one strategy that everyone is aligned with.

In fact, our company *was* growing. When we started out I was an entrepreneur in start-up mode, and all I really cared about was generating revenue: Keep the business going, take on and establish relationships with more and more clients. The difficulty with that is that it leads inevitably to the next phase: "Okay, now I've got to start hiring people." Once that happens, things get *much* more complicated.

Now I have payroll. I have new tax responsibilities associated with the payroll. I have to start tracking not just my work but that of my employees as well. This means more involvement with book-keeping and more meetings with accountants. Like I said, Peter and I each hired our own staff, but responsibility for payroll was entirely in my hands. I was also keeping track of the finances, paying the rent, and meeting the accountant. All of this adds up to more sources of tension.

WHO'S THE BOSS?

ASG had never really had solid leadership, as I discussed in the previous chapter, and in the case of Peter and me, some conflict arose because we did not see eye to eye about who was really in charge. Agreement on leadership—who is the CEO, the final decision maker—is a crucial part of the alignment that should be established between partners up front. Someone has to be in charge and has to be seen by the employees as the person who is in charge.

Since I handled the operations and cut the paychecks, the employees essentially saw me as the president of the company by default. I also had the larger staff and was in the office on a much more regular basis. Peter, as the senior partner in terms of age and experience, did not see it this way.

> Someone has to be in charge and has to be seen by the employees as the person who is in charge.

This produced some awkward situations. At one point, we took our entire staff—still only about seven people—out waterskiing. Peter's wife and son came along, and at one point the son made a comment about how cool it was that his dad was the president of the company and was the boss of all these people. Given the way the staff saw things, this caused some awkward and confused glances to be cast around.

This confirmed, for me, that Peter saw things differently from the way the rest of us did; the kid had to have heard it somewhere, right?

So he saw himself as being in charge—but he wasn't doing the work of actually running the show; and, to top it all off, the value of his 50 percent equity was increasing at the same rate as mine, even though I was managing and paying for most of the staff that was generating that revenue.

This realization, along with the conflict over Madelyn, brought me to the conclusion that I had to do something different somehow. I started by approaching Peter to nudge him in the direction of thinking about strategy, thinking big picture about where he saw himself and the business down the road. I helped him see that our visions were very different. Mine was growth-oriented and would take a lot more work. I wanted to go nationwide and expand beyond just IT recruiting. I even saw an opportunity right in front of us: we were working with a software company that worked predominantly in the pharmaceutical industry, and I wanted to use this connection to migrate into the healthcare and pharmaceutical world, which was, and remains, a much more stable market than IT.

After a couple of discussions like this with Peter, and after consulting with some of my mentors as well as my attorney, I offered to buy him out. He was willing to entertain the idea, and eventually we agreed on a price, and the deal went through. After a three-year partnership—my introduction to the world of business ownership—I was now 100 percent owner and CEO of ASG at age twenty-seven.

This had not been the initial plan, but it is the way things happened, and it led to the start of an even greater adventure. I ended up running ASG for another twenty-four years, in the meantime transforming it into a global oncology contract research organization that provided clinical trial services to biotech and pharmaceutical companies.

As an advisor and longtime business owner, I have seen partnership situations like Peter's and mine play out time and time again: companies not aligned on culture and strategy, not aligned on who was in charge, falling apart. This lack of alignment can also lead (as it did for Peter and me) to one partner taking on all of the operational, payroll, or finance responsibilities, so that, while there may be a 50/50 *equity* partnership, it does not add up to a 50/50 *operational* or *management* partnership. One partner carries most of the weight.

NEGOTIATING THE 50/50 ARRANGEMENT WELL (OR BADLY)

The idea to start a business is often the enthusiastic result of two or three friends, maybe hanging out at a bar, bouncing ideas around one day: "Hey, wouldn't it be cool if we . . ."

This is what happened to my friend Ryan and his business partner, Hank. Ryan and Hank were best friends—they even lived across the street from one another, their wives spent time together, their kids played together, etc. Everything seemed rosy. So Ryan and Hank went into business together, in what seemed like the fairest way possible—50/50. They each owned 50 percent, and they were co-decision makers. You should be able to see where this is going.

One day Ryan called me—he was having trouble with the business. Revenue was down, and he and Hank were starting to have disagreements on strategy. Ryan was frustrated because he felt like he was doing all the work. Hank, who handled operations, wasn't pitching in on the sales side to find new clients, and things were slowing down. They had had to lay some people off, so there was less to do on the operations side, and Ryan felt like he was pulling all the weight.

I told Ryan that, other than liquidating and starting over, which he certainly didn't want to do, he would have to get the money together to buy Hank out, at least to be the majority shareholder so he could be the sole decision maker. Unfortunately, Ryan didn't have the cash, so he was in a tough spot.

Ryan was running into a familiar problem. Many, if not most, business owners form a partnership: partnerships are usually between two people, and most two-person partnerships are 50/50. That seems fair; and what is more straightforward than a 50/50 partnership? But a 50/50 partnership that is 50/50 in terms of *equity* never translates into a partnership that is 50/50 in terms of *responsibility* or *decision making*. As a result, one individual inevitably feels like he or she is the one doing more than the partner. They may even both feel that way because they are looking at things from different sides of the business. Resentment builds, and eventually a crisis point is reached, often even leading to the failure of the business. Problems like this emerge in 50/50 partnerships because these partners dive into the business without taking the time to construct an operating agreement that is independent of just outlining equity shares and that outlines who will be taking responsibility for what.

Think back to those friends at the bar—a lot of times, because they think they're such good friends, they just dive right in. Like Ryan and Hank, they go into it overconfident about how things are going to go—and because their expectations are unrealistic, they fail to plan.

To make things worse, they put themselves into a place where a business going sour would powerfully affect their personal lives. Ryan ultimately incorporated a new company and forced the liquidation of the old one; but, on top of this, he ended up having to move to a new neighborhood after he and Hank separated. A business relationship should not threaten to upend your life. This is why I make it a policy to never do business with close friends.

It is also a good idea to have one partner be the majority shareholder, even if it's a matter of going 51/49, in order to create alignment on who is the final decision maker. Of course, this requires one partner to accept being the *minority* shareholder too. This might seem unlikely, but there are a lot of reasons this might work well. For instance, one party might be the money person, a passive investor who is going to finance most of the business but is fine with leaving the legwork to the other party. More likely is that the one with more cash is going to want to control the money, and the other partner will take a minority share. On the other hand, perhaps one partner just knows their limitations and will happily defer to the other partner.

This strategy avoids the 50/50 equity partnership for the sake of preventing the illusion of a 50/50 split in decision making or responsibility. Of course, the reality is that many, if not most, partnerships will continue to be 50/50. For that reason, business owners should be aware of the pitfalls of this arrangement and head them off as much as possible by constructing an operating agreement. This will set in writing which one of the partners is the ultimate decision maker, the CEO; it will also give a thorough account of each party's roles and responsibilities and the procedures that making decisions in different areas will follow.

Before the first dollar of revenue comes in, this agreement should be worked out so that everyone is on the same page. The operating agreement should take everyone's abilities into account: can the HR person do finances if they need to? If one partner is not a salesperson, can he or she still sell when the company is at a level where everyone needs to be on board with selling? If not, who is going to do these things? If the partners cannot agree on these matters, then they just shouldn't go into business together.

An operating agreement goes beyond a business plan. Ryan and Hank had an agreed-upon strategy, but they didn't work out roles and responsibilities in an operating agreement, and they didn't agree on which one of them would be the CEO. This agreement would have only required the two of them sitting down with an attorney and discussing what they wanted the agreement to contain, and it would have made some of their issues disappear.

> Before the first dollar of revenue comes in, this agreement should be worked out so that everyone is on the same page.

This is another way that a partnership is like a marriage. Some couples go into a marriage riding the high of a new relationship—and these are the ones that fall apart. Couples stay together when they go into it having worked out agreements about whether and how to raise children, for example, as well as how to handle disagreements. The unstable ones can be derailed just by a disagreement on whether or not to have a real Christmas tree.

GETTING IT RIGHT

I recently worked as an advisor to a three-person partnership that was remarkably well designed. Each partner owned one-third of the business. One person was primarily responsible for sales, another for operations and finance, and the third for managing the business.

They had a very good working relationship and the business was successful, in part because everybody knew who had what responsibilities, and everyone knew who the CEO was.

Also, since there were three of them, when a decision had to be made, there would always be a tiebreaker. This suggests another strategy that can also make a 50/50 partnership work better: agree upon a board of directors with an odd number of people on it. A majority would always rule.

This three-person partnership was ultimately able to negotiate a sale of the company that resulted in a lucrative exit for all three of them.

So the key lesson here is that, in spite of 50/50 partnerships being quite common, for better or for worse, these never go hand in hand with an even split in operations, management, responsibility, or decision making. Business owners should be on the lookout to avoid this natural confusion; just because you own half of the company, you don't necessarily make half the decisions.

Like so many other business owners, I learned this lesson the hard way. But when things went awry, I was able to see it through thanks to good advice from mentors and careful attention to how I wanted my business to operate and to grow.

CHAPTER 4

SHADY CHARACTERS

"Phil's not coming in today."

"Why not?"

"Well . . . he's in jail."

That is a conversation you don't want to have about an employee. I had just met with Phil the previous afternoon.

The manager I was talking to had seen his mug shot on the Internet even before Phil's wife called in. My first thought was, "Wait, you look at mug shots every day?" But then I moved past that and inquired further. It turns out Phil, after a night of drinking, had gotten into an argument with his wife and assaulted her. I was stunned—this is not what I expected from my employees.

At the time (the late nineties), we were doing mostly pharmaceutical staffing. I had offices in Connecticut, North Carolina, Illinois, and California. We were doing well—not killing it but growing every single year.

During that period of growth, I had not experienced any difficulties with employees like this one. The company had hiring practices in place that pretty effectively screened out problem employees, and we had a culture that did not condone this kind of behavior. However, we had recently brought on a new team of people, and this had introduced a new element into the company that conflicted with our internal culture and was apparently causing trouble externally as well.

GETTING DISTRACTED, GETTING FOOLED

This trouble with the new team was a side effect of my attempt to move the company into a new line of business that I had been attracted to. Basically, what had happened was that a few of my connections at one of our corporate partners had pitched to me the idea of moving into a new market; they had a plan, and it was going to be tremendous. I was intoxicated by their pitch, so I went in full force. I was thinking emotionally and not analytically; I even went against the advice of my closest advisors and mentors. This got the company in some trouble down the road, including the situation with Phil.

The first step in this process was bringing Alex on board. He was a higher-up at one of our corporate partners, and now he was going to lead our new sales team. He insisted on having me sign an employment contract with him, which I had never done before. It was a three-year contract, and I would have to pay him a hefty extra sum if I fired him during that term "without cause." I assumed, wrongly as it turns out, that poor job performance would count as "cause." I didn't want to take the time to have my attorney take a look at the contract, because it seemed straightforward and unproblematic to me—and I was eager to get started in this new area. So Alex was on board.

We gave Alex everything he wanted—a big office, a nice laptop, a whiteboard in his office. He spent his first few days decorating his office; it got so nice he decided to never leave. He conducted all affairs, including meetings, in his office. Most of his days were spent emailing and hiring more staff—not actually doing any business selling, which was still mostly on the phone in those days. I just figured he knew the ways of this new business sector, so I let him do his thing, assuming it would turn out well down the road.

Over the course of the next three months, he hired more than fifteen people. I had to expand my office space to make room for all these new employees. One of these was Phil.

Phil was supposed to be our primary salesperson, and we had spent a lot of money recruiting him. He was billed as a top-flight salesperson who we definitely wanted on board because he was going to take us to the promised land.

He always had a big deal just on the horizon. But as weeks turned to months, nothing materialized. Suddenly, a year had gone by, and we had spent a lot of money for nothing.

The situation was the same with this whole department; I was being sold a bill of goods. Every day I was being told that a huge project was just around the corner, 75 or 95 percent likely, that was going to bring in big money. Okay, I would say, let's do it. We had the staff and the resources waiting—bring it on. We built it; they had better come.

This had never been the strategy before. We had always been a grow-as-you-go business: if the business came in, then we would hire for it, not the other way around.

In the meantime, resentment was building on the legacy side of our business; they were the engine that was supporting our company, while this new arm of the business so far was just a huge drag on the business. We had hard-working people on the legacy side making sales and generating revenue and corporate "hot shots" on the other side who talked a good game but didn't get anything done. This new tension meant that our culture was changing for the worse.

All of this came to a head one day when I saw one of the new employees sitting at his desk reading the newspaper. I asked him why he wasn't working, and he said he had nothing to do. I confirmed with his manager that he had nothing to do, but the manager insisted that we would need him some day down the line. Of course, if employees have nothing to do, then their managers don't really have anything to do either. As I walked back to my office I realized I had made a mistake—a $1.5 million mistake.

Finally, I hired an outside consultant to come in and do a business assessment. After two weeks, he gave me his report and validated the fact that I was losing money hand over fist and that this whole business unit that we had started was not going to be successful with the people who were currently running it.

So I did what I should have done in the first place—or, really, should never have put myself in the position of having to do—and cut most of the new division, including Alex and Phil.

Alex had put some language in his employment contract that tied his bonuses to the sales on the legacy side of the business, and, after I let him go, I got a letter from an attorney about a month later saying that I owed Alex $500,000, plus bonuses, for firing him "without cause." I was puzzled. He never made any sales—how could I offer him a bonus? Plus, I felt like I had the clearest "cause" in the world to fire him—but the legal fine print suggested otherwise. "I should have gone to my attorney with that contract," I was thinking. We ultimately agreed on a much lower settlement for Alex. My attorney said this was a big win, but I didn't see it that way. From my point of view this had all been a big—and very expensive—error on my part.

BARNACLES AND BULLIES

In this case, I wasn't managing as effectively and decisively as I could have been. This is something business leaders must be on the lookout for. For instance, it is not uncommon for managers or business owners, especially younger ones, to want to be loved by everybody or to be intimidated by or afraid of some of their employees.

Managers that want to be loved are similar to parents who want to be their kids' friends. The problem with this: they never say no. If an employee complains, for instance, the manager is going to try to do right by that person, even if it's not best for the company. There is no discipline, which leads to increasing misbehavior on the part of the kid/employee and lack of control on the part of the parent/manager. The discipline to make tough choices early on saves both a lot of grief down the road.

A manager should not confuse being liked with being respected. A really good leader and manager is going to make decisions that are in the best interest of the business, which leads to respect, even if some people aren't happy in the short run. A manager who is afraid to make a decision that is going to anger or upset the employees in the organization basically enables employees to be unengaged in the values and purpose of the company, which results in underperformance.

One hazard of this type of ineffective management is that it breeds a certain type of employee: the Barnacle. Barnacles are mediocre employees who are good at doing just enough that they hang onto their jobs. They fly below the radar, and they can stay employed for as long as they like, provided they have managers who are afraid or not disciplined enough to make the tough decisions to cut them loose.

> A manager should not confuse being liked with being respected.

The Barnacle is not a cancer to the organization—after all, you can still operate a ship with barnacles on it—and comes across as a team player. But the Barnacle is a drain on the organization. He or she may be late for work on a regular basis or may miss days here and there. He or she sticks around and gets a raise every year but does nothing to really contribute to the profitability of the company.

Still, the Barnacle is not a bad employee. The manager doesn't have a pressing reason to cut him or her, and he or she ends up being able to stick around because the company doesn't have an effective process in place that evaluates employees on a regular basis, that assesses their productivity and communicates that assessment. In other words, the individual employee experiences low *performance pressure.*

Business owners can avoid this hazard, however. Even if a company is too small to have an HR department, it needs an employee handbook, as well as assessment and evaluation processes put in place to assess and encourage employee growth and performance. Such procedures maintain discipline, and managers can use them to monitor the employees under them and help those employees grow within the organization. Without that, the company risks accumulating Barnacles.

In some cases, a business owner or manager is simply intimidated by an employee: the Bully, who uses his or her clout to basically intimidate his or her managers. How can this happen? I recently had a client, a CEO, who ran into a problem with a key employee—or, at least, the client *saw* him as a key employee—in his company. This CEO had been having some conflicts with the other two members of his management team, and he thought that if he could bring in some revenue, they might back off a little bit. So he hired this employee to run the company's business development function. The main office, though, was about a hundred miles from the employee's home, and he wasn't willing to relocate. The company wanted him so badly that they cut a sweetheart deal with him where he was making six figures working from home.

He operated just like Alex and Phil, always promising that a lot of deals were coming down the pipeline. He would become defensive if the CEO ever questioned or pressed him about this, essentially shutting down the CEO, who was too intimidated then to push the salesperson hard. Instead, the CEO went home every night hoping and believing that tomorrow would be the day that the big deal this employee was promising would come through.

The employee, though, was just spinning his wheels. He was not doing his job, and he was able to get away with it for two years due to the fact that the CEO was afraid to just let him go. Finally, after consulting with me, the CEO ended up firing the salesperson, and I helped him set up a daily communication huddle with his two other management folks. I told him, "Don't worry about being the bad guy. Just worry about making a decision. Define that decision and how it's going to be made, but make sure it's defined as what's in the best interest of the business. If you run into conflict, you've just got to keep asking yourself and asking the team that same question over and over again."

But in the meantime, he had lost about $250,000 because he was nervous about standing up to a Bully.

THE ENTERTAINER

During this process, I had the opportunity to look at this key employee's resume. I recognized him right away. He had switched jobs roughly every other year for the previous ten years. This indicated to me that he was a familiar character: the professional interviewee, or, as I like to call him, the Entertainer (after the Billy Joel song). The Entertainer is a high-priced, low-production, high-level executive, typically in business development, sales, or strategy.

Think about it this way: If you're getting a new job every year-and-a-half to two years, then you are probably interviewing at least five to eight times with five to eight different companies every couple of years. You have become really good at developing a resume. You have become really good at interviewing. You have become really good at networking because you are meeting a whole set of new companies and people every two years. You are a superstar on LinkedIn; your profile looks phenomenal.

Keep this in mind too, though: being good at interviewing for a job is not the same as being good at the job. Entertainers are experts at self-branding, not expert at the work they are being hired to do. That brand is going to keep them in their current jobs for about a year and a half; during that time, the folks that hired them are still expecting great things—the great things that the Entertainers promised. After a while, though, the brand starts to erode a little bit for those companies, so the Entertainers go into professional branding mode, gearing up to sell themselves to the next companies willing to take them on. This will typically be a step up also, at least in terms of salary; the Entertainers will come up with very good explanations of why they are leaving their previous companies. Thus, Entertainers obtain career advancement, further enhancing their brands.

What do Entertainers do once they get new jobs? Pick your metaphor: phone it in, tread water, move the chess pieces around. They don't plan to stay in these jobs long term but rather take the jobs because they're more money and they add experience to their resumes. Entertainers thus don't have to work. After they lock down jobs, not much happens except for delay tactics. The businesses, during this time, are definitely sending more money out the door in the form of the Entertainers' salaries than they are bringing in. Most shocking of all is how long companies stick with Entertainers before getting rid of them—two years is typical.

I have heard client after client talk about former employees who fit this profile. The Entertainer typically looks great, always shines in the interview, charms everyone with jokes and humorous anecdotes, treats everyone very familiarly. He or she promises prospects, sales, contacts, and big wins down the road. He or she often thrives off of the inexperience of start-ups or the desperation of struggling companies.

I have even encountered the Entertainer in my own business. In the last years of my ownership at Ockham, we began recruiting for the position of high-end technical advisor for one of our service offerings. Ron popped up on our radar, and from a background per-spective he seemed perfect. He had the right degrees, and he had experience in oncology, which is the area we were working in. He was not employed at the time because, he claims, his previous company had been having massive layoffs, and he had graciously done the company a favor by taking the severance package and bowing out. Two years prior to that he had been with still another company—where he had also stayed for just about two years. We could see this on his resume, but it didn't raise a red flag for us as it should have.

Within his first few weeks, he joined the company at a major conference where we would be meeting with clients and entertaining them. The plan was to roll out the new guy's expertise to help the clients and help drum up further business down the road. We would all be having breakfast and dinner with clients from Saturday through Tuesday.

So we started with dinner on Saturday night, and Ron was with us. The next morning he was with us for breakfast and then exhibited with us through lunch. After lunch he said he needed to do some work in his room, so we planned to see him again that evening at dinner. Around 7 p.m., he emailed saying he wasn't going to be able to make dinner, as he had too much work to do. I was not thrilled about this; we were all ready to go, to present him to this client, who was looking forward to meeting this new guy. But we couldn't do anything but move on without him.

The next day, he didn't show up for breakfast—same for lunch. Midafternoon he appeared at the booth and explained that he had worked all day Sunday and then decided to turn in early and sleep in the next morning so he could be fresh for Monday evening.

"Oh my God," I thought, "I'm not paying this guy a considerable six-figure salary so he can sleep through a whole day of a four-day conference." Then I started to notice that, in talking to clients, he clearly thought he was the smartest person in the room. He didn't listen to clients' ideas or needs, and the ideas he served up were out of date. He wasn't up with the latest technology; basically, he was just resting on his laurels.

On the flight home, it dawned on me that I had been duped by the Entertainer. Only then did I see the red flags on his resume: for the past fifteen years, he had been jumping from job to job before landing on us, where he thought he could cool his heels for a while.

He hadn't counted on our having a conference just a few weeks after hiring him. He thought he could handle the conference, but the experience quickly revealed that his values and his work ethic were not aligned with what we expected of our employees, especially at the top level. This exposed him early, and we were able to get rid of him.

The Entertainer is always going to stand out as the best-qualified candidate, from his or her background to the way he or she interviews. What companies have to do is look at that person's resume and think not, "Wow, this person has a lot of experience" but rather, "Wow, this person has been at five jobs in the last six to ten years. Why in the world would he or she stay at my place for more than a year to two years?" Then they should tell the Entertainer, "Thanks, but no thanks."

STAYING FOCUSED

Apart from Ron, we very rarely hired people from the outside for top-level positions. We always promoted from within. In deviating from this, we made a serious and expensive error—just as we had done with Alex and his team earlier.

In that earlier case, as I mentioned, the mistake lay in my losing focus on what had allowed for the growth of the company up to that point in time: our existing employees, our workplace culture, and our hiring practices. For hiring salespeople, in particular, what had worked in the past was providing a large, incentive-based compensation package. Employees received about 30 percent base salary, with the rest made up of variable compensation and commission. If they were passionate and engaged and believed in the market, they would be knocking it out of the park in three to six months, even if they had taken a pay cut coming in.

In taking on this new business line, we were talked out of this model by our corporate partner: "You're never going to get a good salesperson in this industry for that kind of compensation package." We just had to have these people, so we broke with tradition. We gave them a compensation package where 90 percent was nonvariable. The result? We didn't make any sales on that side of the business.

We also had never had employment contracts. With Alex, we did—and that came back to bite us, too.

If we had stuck to our core KPI structure for human resources, we would have smoked these people out within two or three interviews, and we wouldn't have hired them. They wouldn't have come on board, and we would have never taken the chance to pursue this market.

That would have been better in the long run. I shouldn't have gone down that road in the first place. I had led the company into deviating from our path in hiring and away from our culture and core values. I went against the advice of my trusted employees, managers, and mentors. I got sucked into a decision based on feeling alone and not on actual analytical data. I didn't want to make the tough decisions, so I allowed guys like Phil and Alex to stay around a lot longer than I should have.

Everything we did in this situation was the exact opposite of what had been successful for us prior to that. If you have a well-worn hiring process that works, don't deviate from it when you're trying to get into a new market. In situations like that, all that happens is that companies compromise their values, they are slow to make decisions that are in the best interest of business, and they erode the capital that they have accumulated with the good employees in the organization. Those employees then tend to become disgruntled and/or walk out the door.

On the other hand, a company that engages its employees, that stays true to its mission and core values, will retain good employees. Surveys conducted by organizations like TINYpulse have shown repeatedly that the number-one reason for turnover is employee engagement. It is not money.[1] It is not benefits. It is not job title. It is employee engagement.

If employees know and believe in the mission and the values of the organization, and if the leadership stays true to those values, then employees will be more loyal than if that company just paid them more money without further engaging them. Companies need to work to develop such a culture, as well as to put in place systems of assessing and then rewarding or censuring employees, to put some performance pressure on them.

A company that engages its employees, that stays true to its mission and core values, will retain good employees

Employees can be quite costly if business owners do not adequately focus on what is best for the company or if they lack the discipline to make difficult decisions or design rigorous hiring and assessment practices. If owners do this correctly, however, they will ensure that employees play a crucial role in securing the success of the business.

---

1 Victor Lipman, "Why Do Employees Leave Their Jobs? New Survey Offers Answers," accessed April 19, 2017, www.forbes.com/sites/victorlipman/2015/10/10/why-do-employees-leave-their-jobs-new-survey-offers-answers/#414f2f356a90.

CHAPTER 5

ASSESSING VALUE

Basically, Justin had just walked in and smacked me in the face. Not literally, of course—though I might have preferred that to what he did do, which was walk into my office, sit down across the desk from me, and say, "You know you're not making any money, right?"

That can't be right, I thought; but it was. He showed me how the numbers worked out. It turns out I had been misled by bad financial data, and I was using that data to run the business. I had thought my gross margin was about 30 percent per revenue-generating employee, but when he ran the numbers more thoroughly he showed me that it was closer to 18 percent. Then throw in rent and non-revenue-generating employees, and at the end of it I was barely breaking even.

This was seven years into my ownership of ASG. Prior to hiring Justin as CFO, I had still been using the same software platform I had started with. I had worked out the tax situation early on, and we were in compliance with all the regulatory agencies and the IRS, so

I wasn't meeting with an accountant all that regularly. According to the books as I had been keeping them (specifically, on a cash basis rather than an accrual basis), the business was profitable. I wasn't sure what the value of the business was exactly—I wasn't thinking about exiting anytime soon—but I was sure it was pretty solid. We were growing every year, and I thought we were on top of the world.

At the same time, though, I was plugging in all the financial data to the computer, basically doing the books, entirely on my own. I hated doing it, quite frankly, and I'm not an expert in everything; so I had hired Justin as CFO so that he could come in and take over that side of the business, take everything off my hands, and make sure our finances were functioning appropriately.

What he had done was review the financials, walk into my office, and throw a wrench into my whole plan for the growth of the business. I had been operating with bad data with no financial mentor looking over my shoulder for *seven years*; I had thought all was going well, until I brought someone in to check on it who ended up telling me I was on the wrong track.

Fortunately, I was willing to listen, and that is when the adventure began. With Justin's help, I was able to turn the company around and get it back to a state of growth and profitability. I had again learned the hard way about the importance of good financial data, about the key role of the financial gatekeeper (in this case, Justin), and most of all about the perils of not assessing the value of your business objectively.

A SKEWED VIEW

It is all too easy, in fact, to evaluate the value of your business *subjectively*. This is the error that one of our acquisitions targets, CEO Julia, had made, which ultimately led to her sending me an email out of the blue: "Hey, it's been a while. Can we talk?" I was happy to talk with her that very afternoon, and before long I heard what I was expecting to hear: "So, uh . . . is that offer still on the table?"

Almost a full year prior, my company had offered to buy Julia's company, which, like my company, was offering research services in the healthcare arena. She was sure at the time, however, that we were greatly undervaluing her business. Unfortunately, she was misguided on that very issue; she didn't have the proper financial guidance to really take stock of what the value of the company was. Our review of her financials revealed that she was in debt and operating at a loss. I still thought we could benefit from the purchase of her company, but our offer ended up being much lower than she hoped. She turned down our offer.

Now she was contacting me out of desperation: she was going through a divorce, she was under a crushing debt load, and the IRS was after her. She was coming back to us with the realization that our offer had been more generous than she had thought. Sadly, by that time, it would have made no sense for us to buy her out. Ultimately, she filed for bankruptcy and the company was liquidated.

What had gone wrong? Julia had taken a crucial misstep in valuing her company subjectively, without outside guidance or input and without the proper data and metrics. As a result, her estimate of her company's value was far greater than what the market was telling her (in the form of the offer we made to buy the company). Instead of taking this as a sign that she needed to rethink how she was looking at her financial situation, she decided that the *market* was the one getting it wrong; so she kept going down the same path she was on, which turned out to be a downward spiral, in value terms.

Her plans for exit from the company did not turn out how she expected. If she had viewed the initial market response as a reality check, leading her to reevaluate her financials, then she might have been able to reorient the business in a new and more profitable direction. Instead, she stuck to the plan, and it did not end well for her.

Julia, like many business owners, had really paid attention only to the revenue her company was bringing in when estimating the value of her business. She was not adequately taking into account the amount of cash flowing out or the debt that the business was saddled with. The market, however, *does* take account of those things. What she *saw* as profit (incoming revenue) would not be reflected as profit in the marketplace, given the countervailing expense and debt.

Debt, in particular, is going to decrease the amount a company can be sold for in the marketplace, with the result that the business owner gets a disappointing sum at closing. Of course, if your company is valued at $5 million, but you have $1 million of debt, then you're going to net $4 million, thus coming away at closing with 20 percent less than the value of the company.

Julia was in even worse shape—her debt actually outweighed her profitability, *and* marketizing her financials (using standard financial reporting accepted in her market) showed that she was actually losing money. From that point of view, the offer my company had made was in fact overly generous; she would have been able to get out with some value from her equity in the company and pay off a lot of her personal debt as well.

Our offer, however, bruised her ego, and she rejected our offer and stuck to her old strategy. This is a common mistake, based primarily on an ignorance of how to measure the value of a company in the marketplace, as well as, sometimes, an unwillingness to even address that lack of knowledge. These bad habits or misguided practices are in the long run harmful to an owner's chances to achieve a positive exit from that business.

A valuable business is going to be strong in all areas; it must be able to sell and deliver quality to its customers or clients, and it must have good employees and thus good HR practices. What a lot of business owners neglect, though, is strength in the area of financial fundamentals. This requires a process in place to recognize revenue, account for expense, and ultimately recognize profit in a way that's acceptable to the marketplace that company is in.

Of course, many business owners have a finance background, and they are much more likely to avoid these pitfalls. Many entrepreneurs and small business owners, though, do not have that knowledge, and they tend to focus on either generating revenue or delivering quality at the expense of profit. They never really focus on the general accounting and financial principles they need as discipline and guidance in order to run their businesses.

Having those basics in place tells you how much money is going in and coming out at all times, so you always know how much profit you're making per project or product. That data can then be used to improve quality and productivity across the business as well.

SENSE AND NONSENSE

Many business owners, in looking to data that skews the value of their company, are like news consumers who fall for fake news stories; they have missed the reality of the situation, often with disastrous consequences. What is it that they are looking at?

They will look at their financials every few months—monthly, if they are disciplined—but in the meantime, all they are looking at is money in the bank. The better-informed among them will look at earnings before interest, tax, depreciation, and amortization (EBITDA)—or at least the less-fancy "operating profit"—but even that is only suitable as a starting point, not the be-all-end-all measure of value. Furthermore, every once in a while, owners may go to seminars where speakers who want to take advantage of them tell them they can get ten or even fifteen times EBITDA in their market, when in reality they can only get four to six. Combine that inflated multiple with undisciplined financials, and a business owner can walk around thinking that he or she will get ten times more for their company than he or she will actually be able to.

Once this mentality is embedded, an offer for the company that is substantially below the imagined amount comes across like a slap in the face. It is up to you, though, whether you treat it as the kind of slap that insults you or the kind that wakes you up. The smart business owner will take the latter approach and step back and say, "How did this happen?" He or she will treat it as a learning experience. The owner who has fallen for the fake news, like Julia, will walk away with a bruised ego and continue down an unproductive or even destructive path.

Good data is crucial to assessing the value of a business and potentially from there increasing that value. Building a foundation of good financial data allows you to use that data as the primary metric that drives the business from the market perspective.

If bad data is like fake news, then good data can be compared to the lab results you get after going to the doctor. When you go to the doctor and get lab tests done, every item that those lab tests measure is measured against a standard of health. These standards give a reliable indication of what health looks like and what your condition is in relation to them. When you get good lab results, you are happy and feel like you can conquer the world. The same holds true for businesses that have strong financials.

Putting in place an accounting system that accurately captures these measures, though, can be difficult for entrepreneurs or small business owners, who often start out small. They may not even want a huge company but just a lifestyle business that is an extension of their passions or interests and that they don't necessarily treat as completely distinct from their personal lives. As a result, when they start keeping the books, they use the same method, often a software platform, that they use to manage their personal budget. Many of these software platforms give users the opportunity to upgrade to a business version, which makes that transition all that much easier.

As companies grow, however, these extensions of personal budgeting tools, which are often pretty rudimentary, become totally inadequate; and the sooner an owner realizes that his or her business needs to adopt a new system, the better. Unfortunately, though, many owners don't realize this until it is too late, and the tools they are using have started giving them results that are unreliable, simply because the accounting method of a personal budget is not adequate to the management of the finances of a growing company.

Think back to those lab tests at the doctor. There are metrics of health that we can easily measure at home on our own—weight, heart rate, maybe blood pressure—and these are useful, but they give us an incomplete picture. If we want to really dig in, then we go get the lab work done. We depend on a more sophisticated set of measurements. Similarly, the suped-up checkbooks that we use for personal budgeting and then for our new small businesses do a great job of keeping track of how much cash is in the bank at any given time; but growing businesses need a more sophisticated system.

Therefore, in all cases, it is important to understand your "lab measurements" in your market. If you own food trucks, chances are you will be on a cash accounting basis. If you are in the building business or providing a long-term service, then you should be on an accrual-based accounting system. The cash system counts a customer's or client's payment of an invoice as revenue at the time the business receives the payment, whether this is before or after the work or the product being paid for has been delivered.

> The sooner an owner realizes that his or her business needs to adopt a new system, the better.

In accrual-based accounting, incoming cash is counted as revenue after work or the product is delivered, whether or not it has been paid for; it thus more clearly indicates profit per deliverable for whatever industry the company is in. This gives a more accurate picture of the financial state of a business; perhaps more importantly, most markets will measure performance by reading standardized accrual-based financials. In most cases, it is thus in the best interest of any business owner who hopes to have a successful exit to move to an accrual-based system. Rather than get into the details of how this accrual-based accounting works, however, I'll just recommend seeking out a quality financial advisor, or even hiring one full time if you have the capability. Such advisors will be able to help you measure and value your business more effectively.

After all, when we look at our lab results, we don't really know what we're looking at until we have a trained professional, a doctor, come in and explain them to us. We don't think we're experts on the results just because it's *our* body. Why, then, do business owners presume to act like the financial experts in their own businesses instead of bringing in or hiring on trained expertise to help them take measurements and take stock of what those measurements say about their business's health?

THE IMPORTANCE OF A GATEKEEPER

Most businesses, at least if they're large enough to have hired employees outside of a very small circle, have a bookkeeper—and someone serving in this capacity is crucial. However, in addition to this, a company needs a financial *gatekeeper*: not necessarily a CFO but at least someone who will provide a second pair of eyes, from a financial perspective, on company decisions about implementing strategy and managing operations going forward. A good gatekeeper should be invested in the financial health of the business, so that they will look out for the company's best interests and be willing to tell the leadership no and give them constructive criticism.

As I discussed at the beginning of this chapter, I learned this lesson the hard way. ASG was financially vulnerable at the time I hired Justin, due to my inadequate (cash-based) accounting methods and my neglect in seeking financial advice. Justin's insight as CFO, however, reoriented my focus; in particular, he helped me to understand our gross margins in such a way that we were able to shift away from some clients and some service offerings that were not as profitable as others. Justin's financial insight also helped the company identify our key performance indicators (KPIs), which are any positive business indicators you can follow to determine the health of your business: your target gross margin, your average contract length, etc.

In all, then, Justin really served, as a good CFO should, as the gatekeeper for our strategy and operations going forward. By bringing in some good advice from the outside, and focusing on the right data, I was able to avoid Julia's fate.

Again, many companies will not be able to afford the investment in a CFO, but they should still have someone in this financial mentorship role. My advice is, as a first step for a new and growing business, to use an accounting firm that's focused mostly on the tax side. Once you are staying out of trouble from the tax perspective, the next step is to hire an advisor or put someone on the board who has experience in growing a business and can offer significant guidance and advice on how best to run the financial side of the business, in conjunction with the accountant.

It is not uncommon for an entrepreneur to think he or she is the smartest person in the room. However, he or she cannot be omnipresent or be the expert in every aspect of running a business. Outside help is essential, as is receptivity on the part of the business owner. I've seen many business owners kick their accountants out the door for being naysayers; basically, the boss doesn't like what he or she is hearing, so out the accountant goes. This is a mistake; listening is an important skill in itself. A really smart owner knows his or her strengths and weaknesses and then seeks advisors to shore up those weaknesses.

A smart owner also knows to look for outside help and the best data in understanding his or her company's market value—which may not be the same as what the owner subjectively thinks. Confusing these two is one of the most dangerous mistakes a business owner can make—as Julia's story indicates. Knowing the value of the company is key to knowing how healthy the company is overall.

One key component of this health is indicated by gross margin—the measure of how much value a company gets from a product or service in relation to the cost of producing or delivering that product or service. A financial gatekeeper, by identifying gross margin and ways to increase it, can not only protect the company but can also be crucial to growing the business's value in the future.

CHAPTER 6

RECOGNIZING VALUE

September 2007: I was at a meeting in Ireland—it was my first time in the country—and it was snowing. I was very tired after an overnight flight, and as I was listening to the proceedings, I gazed out the window at the snow, which came down heavily for about five minutes before it started raining. What I was seeing, though, was still more pleasant than what I was hearing. The CFO for a potential buyer for ASG was poring over financial data, and all I could think was, "This is about to go south."

Several months before, ASG had been approached by a strategic buyer—a company that was looking to purchase another business with the purpose of accelerating their business strategy. Strategic buyers are often willing to pay more than a business would normally command on the open market. We were interested in this opportunity, which coaxed us into taking a good hard look at our financials. After all, we knew they would ask us for everything under the sun— three years of backdated financial reports, tax returns, any relevant documentation, etc. We would also have to provide a forecast, based on our current billing and costs, adding up to our average gross margin, projected over the next several years.

We had sent our forecast to our investment banker to deliver to the buyer. Soon after, I was supposed to take my family to Italy. On a rainy Tuesday afternoon at the Raleigh-Durham airport, family in tow, flight delayed, I was not in a great mood; and I got a call from my CFO: "I think I screwed up."

"What do you mean?" I said.

"I just looked back over my formulas for calculating gross margin, and one formula was a little off, which caused an error down the line; the gross margin we sent the buyer is about three points higher than it actually is at the moment."

Still at the airport, I called the banker to update him: our gross margin—our revenue minus our cost of goods sold—was off by a few percentage points. That may not sound like much, but if those numbers add up to millions in dollars, plus the multiple we're getting on the sale—that turns out to be a lot of money. It was important to me that the buyer not think we misled them.

The banker, though, was not terribly troubled: "If you have future business coming in that's higher gross margin, then the forecast is going to be updated soon anyway, so let's just leave it, it won't be a big deal." In other words, we could sell more business at a higher gross margin down the line in order to make up for the shortfall on the spreadsheet. We would have to reforecast in a few more months, and if we were successful the formula error would be moot.

Unfortunately, that is not how things turned out—we did not add business with higher gross margins. My trip to Ireland was a couple of months later. Their CFO was going line by line, scrutiniz-ing every single number, and he and I were both picking up on the fact that our gross margins weren't as strong as they wanted them to be. At that point I realized that it would take a miracle for the deal to go through. When you start praying for miracles in business, it is time to face reality and accept that the deal will die unless you are willing to accommodate a reduced price. In this case, I wasn't.

THE IMPORTANCE OF GROSS MARGIN

So the deal did not go through, but it did turn out to be another turning point for the company. On the path we had been following, we were going to be indefinitely stuck at the point where we were— no growth, no upward trajectory in gross margin. Gross margin is a percentage measurement that expresses, basically, how much a company makes on each of its deliverables: take the price that the product or service is sold for, subtract the *cost* of delivering that product or service, and calculate the difference as a percentage of price. If you sell a widget for $10, for example, and that widget cost you $7 to produce, you make a gross profit of $3—your gross margin is 30 percent.

Our gross margin was starting to dwindle; put simply, we found ourselves in the unenviable position of doing more work but creating less income. The failure of this sale turned out to be the beginning of a new adventure that involved hard work and reflection on what areas of service and what clients were giving us the highest margin—our "crown jewels," as I call them. We reworked our strategy to address those areas and those clients more and to move away from the ones that were dragging our margin down.

As the story of my attempt to sell the company shows, gross margin is a crucial measure of the financial health and profitability of a company and can have a decisive effect on how that company is valued in the marketplace. Running a successful business with a chance of a lucrative exit thus requires close attention to gross margin. How much are you making on your product or service per unit sold?

Attention to gross margin can lead to the discovery of a company's crown jewels, as it did in the case of ASG. For example, a company might have a crown jewel in terms of client base. If a company has a particular client that it is getting a high gross margin from, then that company may have found its crown jewel. The owners would then be well advised to try to provide more value for that client, as well as to pursue other clients in the same market or pursue the trends that that client represents.

For instance, as we examined our gross margins after the sale of our company did not go through in 2007, we realized that oncology research was delivering our highest margins; so we started shifting toward a focus on oncology and away from other types of medical research. By the time I sold the company, seven years later, we were an oncology-only CRO and functional service provider (i.e., a high-end, specialized staffing company)—and my exit ended up being more successful than I had ever hoped.

Companies can also strategically increase gross margins from their existing client base in a variety of ways. Some pricing structures, for instance, will deliver higher margins than others, depending on the nature of the industry. Would it be more beneficial to charge a flat fee than an adjustable rate based on time and materials, for example? You need to know how much a product or project costs to deliver and structure your pricing so as to maximize the margin. This might seem obvious; but given that the financial fundamentals are neglected by so many business owners, these strategic considerations are often overlooked as well.

> Gross margin is a crucial measure of the financial health and profitability of a company and can have a decisive effect on how that company is valued in the marketplace.

It is also very common for owners to miss out on ways to cut the cost of a deliverable while actually delivering the same quality. For instance, often a job can be done just as well by a less-experienced (and thus cheaper) employee. An owner might brag about the high-end IT guy with twenty years of experience he or she has on his team; but that owner must consider what the client is actually looking for. If it's IT services that can be performed just as well by his other IT person, who has just four years of experience and demands $20,000 a year less, then put that other person on the job. The margin then explodes, since the owner is paying much less to deliver, while still charging the client the same amount. Gross margin can explode in several such ways once owners start paying attention and finding ways to cut costs.

WHAT IS YOUR CROWN JEWEL?

Understanding gross margin allows business owners to understand a more fundamental question: What makes their business *valuable?* What is the thing—the product or the service—that clients are willing to pay good money for? This is a business's crown jewel in terms of value. A company's strategy should always be to focus, and build the business around, that crown jewel. This in turn results in the identification and pursuit of the key performance indicators (KPIs) that are best for that business.

For ASG, which started as a staffing company and morphed into a CRO, the crown jewel was oncology research. This is why we ultimately became an *oncology* CRO, which maximized our value so that my exit went very well.

There had been previous times when I lost sight of my business's crown jewel—for instance, when I brought on Alex and the troublesome new team that I discussed in chapter 4. I had been attracted to a new market and tried to move our service offering horizontally into a new area. What happens when decisions like this are made without looking closely at the business's crown jewels is that the value of the business gets watered down. The business stagnates or even starts sinking.

If a business is delivering a value, then the owners can also reflect on their client base: are the clients they currently have the best clients for them, or could they produce higher gross margins with different clients? To use my own company as an example: ASG (later Ockham) specialized in early-stage clinical trials. We were good at them, and they were the most profitable for us. Would it have been beneficial for us to secure a huge client in the pharmaceutical industry such as Pfizer? The answer is most likely no for two reasons.

The first relates to our crown jewel: Phase I and Phase II trials in the oncology sector. Trials are usually at Phase III before big companies like Pfizer snatch them up. Doing Phase III trials for Pfizer would mean pursuing a horizontal move to another area of service, putting the profitability of our crown jewel in jeopardy.

A company's strategy should always be to focus and build the business around that crown jewel.

Second: let's say that Pfizer happens to be interested in a Phase I or Phase II trial, and they approach us. For a company that size, a company the size of mine is just a cog in a wheel, part of an overall outsourcing model. Pfizer would not fully appreciate the special value of having ASG/Ockham as their CRO. We could pat ourselves on the back for having such a big player as a client, but ultimately a company that size is not going to value our service at the level it might be valued elsewhere. That is, they might only be willing to pay us a 25 percent gross margin; while, on the other hand, a start-up biotech or pharmaceutical firm that has raised a lot of money and is looking for the best CRO to do their Phase I trials would happily pay margins of 40 or 45 percent for our expertise. In that case, it would be best to maintain our client focus and not look to land a much bigger client.

Business owners thus need to pay close attention to which members of their client base are valuing them more, as well as what they are valued for. Many businesses would eagerly take a big, reliable client, since that means the safety net of repeat business. In fact, I recently advised a company that provided about 90 percent of their services to a single client. That's a lot of repeat business! It also meant that that client had a stranglehold on company strategy— all decisions were made with an eye to providing the best value to a *single client*. This is a recipe for broader market irrelevance and eventual stagnation.

Furthermore, that one client expected them to provide that repeat service year after year for the same price. At the same time, year after year the employees expect, and receive, pay increases. The result is that costs go up while price stays the same, thus consistently dropping gross margins, creating a precarious situation. This company obviously needed to diversify its client base.

Company leaders often get caught up in spending the majority of their time thinking about revenue creation and growth, only to lose sight of the current sources of their successful business. Understanding your most profitable clients—and what they are buying from you—adds business value. Business value can be compromised or even lost when there is a lack of focus on the value for which your clients are paying.

Understanding this means taking a deep dive on the business's KPIs from the financial perspective of (1) what kind of product or service you're delivering, (2) to what kind of client, and (3) with what level of employee involved in the delivery? By doing this, a business owner can advance from *understanding* the level of financial health of their business, as we discussed in the previous chapter, to actually increasing that health in the form of exploding gross margins. As I mentioned, this process requires a good financial advisor, and seeking advice from mentors is also always a good measure.

DISCIPLINE

Once a business owner has discovered his or her company's crown jewels and KPIs, the next step is to maintain discipline. The owner should not deviate from these core value-adding principles.

ASG's decision to focus only on oncology resulted from a bad experience in deviating from our crown jewels. Against the wishes of some of the leadership, we had bid on a clinical study for muscular dystrophy, and we ended up winning, even though we actually had no experience in that area of research at all. The sales team was happy about it; if it went well, we could make a decent profit.

We first faced the problem of patient recruitment, which was made more difficult than normal due to the fact that this was a pediatric study. To add to the difficulty, the client, which was a start-up running a study for the first time, was being extremely difficult and very demanding. They criticized our patient recruitment efforts and complained about the qualifications of our project managers. This soon developed into a perfect storm of a difficult research area in which we had no experience, a difficult client, and a difficult patient recruitment process.

That storm hit us like a ton of bricks one day a few months into the study. The client called to ask our team, including the senior leadership, to meet at their site—and at our expense. We arrived, only to be promptly fired. We had never been dropped from a study before; this hurt. We lost morale, we lost money, and our reputation with this new client wouldn't recover.

As a result, from that day forward the leadership at Ockham made the decision to focus solely on oncology research. That was where our value lay. Of course, we had clients calling up our salespeople and asking us to do other studies. The salespeople, of course, wanted to make as many sales as possible, so the leadership kept getting pressure from sales to take on other types of studies. Of course, it's difficult to turn down business; but that is ultimately what we did.

Why was that the right decision? Why not take some of the low-hanging fruit in much simpler and low-cost areas. The market in these areas, for this very reason, was highly competitive, while the oncology market was much more selective and the studies much more complex. As a result, we could find a very high value in specializing in oncology; we would have benefitted very little from doing other, more readily available types of studies that we wouldn't have been the most qualified firm for anyway.

> Not all business is good business, and in fact it can be detrimental when it serves to water down the value of the company.

Still, as I said, it is hard to turn down business; staying focused like this requires a lot of discipline on the part of a company's leadership. Not all business is *good* business, and in fact it can be detrimental when it serves to water down the value of the company. Just as a company must stay true to its core values and its culture, so it must also stay true to its KPIs and its crown jewels. These go hand in hand in leading a business to success.

CHAPTER 7

MISSION, PASSION, MARKETING

" **A** nd that's what brought me to Ockham." Katherine looked around at the roomful of people she had been addressing; I'm sure what she saw made quite an impression. After all, it's not something you see every day, especially at an annual corporate meeting: a crowd of emotional people sniffling and wiping tears from their eyes. I was emotional myself, and I led my colleagues in a round of applause for Katherine's deeply affecting presentation.

The theme for the annual meeting that year was "Our People, Our Purpose," linking our employees to our mission as an oncology research firm—nearly everyone has been touched by cancer in some way or another. Katherine had volunteered to tell her story. She started by showing a slide of her mom, who had been a very active, athletic, robust individual with a loving family before suddenly developing a brain tumor. Over the next half hour, Katherine told the story of her mom's diagnosis and treatment, then the family's realization that she was not going to survive, and finally her mother's passing away.

She connected this to her own decision to leave a previous job to go into the world of oncology research, which had brought her to our company.

Katherine was the best business development employee I've ever seen. She had come on board when we purchased her employer's company, Nexus, an oncology CRO where she had been in sales. Katherine had sold in other industries, but she had been new to the oncology sector when she started at Nexus and had ended up playing the role less of a salesperson and more of an administrator on steroids—that is, she drummed up business for the boss by reaching out and setting up meetings. Ultimately, the company's CEO was making all the final sales.

We put Katherine in business development when we acquired Nexus, with a better salary plus commission. This turned out to be the right decision; her potential was just not being realized at Nexus. When she came to us, she ran with the job and thrived in the environment we provided, ultimately doing spectacular work.

She was also very engaging and had a special skill for getting through to people—which, of course, is how she was able to bring a roomful of people to tears. The scene was remarkable in itself, but it made something else hit home for me as well: Katherine had gotten into this line of work to help companies find cures for cancer, to save other moms like her own down the road. She wasn't the business owner; she hadn't gone out to start up her own new business. She was an employee who had been working in one sector, had a personal tragedy, and decided to pursue work in another sector entirely. Her drive in her new job, and her success, was motivated by a personal sense of *mission*.

This provides a perfect example of the profound influence that a company's mission can have on an employee, as well as how passionate employees—the people that make a company successful—are the drivers of that mission. If employees are passionate and have a sense of being engaged and having a purpose, then the company benefits from the bottom up—the owners can feed off of that passion, and they can use it to enhance and drive the culture, and even the marketing, of the company.

A SENSE OF MISSION

Mission concerns the most fundamental question a business owner can (and should) ask himself or herself: *Why are you doing what you're doing?* It is crucial for leaders to operate with a clear answer to this question in mind; it is wise to devote time to crafting a mission statement that captures the purpose that is held not just by the leader but by the employees in an organization. However, don't spend time wordsmithing the mission statement. Simply look in the mirror and listen to your employees and clients, and you will find your mission.

Some business owners might think, "Easy for this guy to say. He ran a cancer research firm! I don't imagine identifying a mission was too hard for him!" This is partly true—it is more straightforward to identify a purpose for an oncology research firm than it might be for other great businesses, such as Uber or a residential cleaning service. However, there are two problems with this view: first, having a mission that is easy to identify doesn't mean that that mission is well articulated and lived inside the company; and second, a business owner can find a mission no matter what sector he or she is in—it may just take harder work to articulate it and to keep employees engaged and passionate.

The strategy for discovering those harder-to-articulate missions is to humanize the service or product the company offers. Take the example I just mentioned of a housecleaning business. What benefit does the business deliver to the client or customer? Well, a clean house—but dig deeper. What does the customer get from a clean house? Perhaps a healthier environment and an overall better quality of life. What might be the employee's perspective on this? What is the mission in what they do, what they accomplish by coming in to work every day (beyond earning a paycheck)? The business owner should brainstorm responses to these questions with the employees, perhaps making suggestions such as: "You make people's lives better. Maybe they're working their tails off at their job, then wrangling the kids, and they just don't have time to clean. You make it possible to have a higher quality of life in a healthier environment and to spend more time with their families, too." The employees can then develop something they can say to themselves, a sort of motto or mantra, to remind them of their mission going forward and enable them to come in and do the best possible job every day.

Whatever that mission is, it must be engrained in the business both from the bottom up and the top down. Nexus provides a good example of this: it was started by Clare, who had been motivated to work in cancer research from a young age after losing her grandfather to cancer. She and Katherine, then, from their different places in the company, still shared the same mission, and this kind of alignment contributes to the success of a company.

Even ASG changed significantly for the better because of this type of self-examination on the part of the leadership. Prior to the attempted sale in 2007, which I discussed in chapter 6, our mission had been focused around financial considerations and the market: growing the company, increasing gross margins. During that earlier period, I always thought we were doing well, but in hindsight I now see that things could have been so much better in so many ways.

In particular, we had pretty consistent turnover among revenue-generating employees—the researchers—because they couldn't connect the mission of the company to what they were doing on a daily basis.

Once we started reflecting on our crown jewels and KPIs, however, a lightbulb came on for us: "We're going to focus on oncology clinical trials. Our goal is to save lives." Once we reached that point, alignment on our mission fell into place. This also allowed us to acquire Clare's CRO, Nexus; Clare had been approached by other buyers, but she was determined that her mission would stay alive even after she sold the company. From Clare's perspective, her dedication to a specific mission made her see clearly what the intrinsic value of her company was, with the result that her M&A strategy worked out smoothly. I connected with her, since we both had lost our fathers to cancer; we were able to share that sense of mission, and it just made sense for us to move forward together.

THE LEADER'S ROLE

Companies often have an engrained, default way of doing things, where the company is focused entirely on the market. This results in a lack of employee engagement. For example, at ASG prior to the turn to oncology, we recruited revenue-generating employees with competitive salaries and an a la carte menu of quality benefits. After they were hired, we had kept track of their time to try to make sure they were staying happy, but we weren't taking initiative on discussing questions like, "Where do we want this person to be with the company five years from now?" or, "What should this person know about the company that will make him or her excited to get up and go to work in the morning?" or even, "How can we get our employees enthusiastic enough about the company to sell it to others, to make referrals?" Also, these employees worked on jobsites rather than in our offices, so they were not integrated into the company's culture. As I mentioned, we also had a good deal of turnover among these employees.

As I mentioned in chapter 4, many surveys have shown that employee engagement and the culture of the company are the strongest factors affecting employee turnover. If a company does what we did and prioritizes compensation and benefits, then they are missing the boat. If a business owner focuses solely on operational or financial matters, he or she is missing out at least half of what he or she should be doing for the company in terms of leadership. Business leaders lead the development of the vision for their companies, which in turn sets the tone for the operations of the companies. Employees want to work for an organization that is growing in a positive direction, and making that positive direction manifest is the job of the leader.

Business owners often think they know the most about a business because it is *theirs*; they started it and they know the market better and so forth—they are the smartest people in the room. This is a mistake. What got them to the position they are in does not necessarily have to do with being smart. It has to do with making the right decisions at the right time and with staying disciplined; but it also has a lot to do with luck and with knowing the right people—both employees and mentors—who can help out along the way.

This becomes even truer as a business grows. Early on, with a start-up, owners are more likely to be out in the field, in the market, meeting with customers. As the business grows, though, owners hire other people to do those jobs. As a result, they become more insulated from what is happening on the ground, like a piece of software that isn't getting updated and ends up inadequate to the new problems that are put to it. When you are not going out into the marketplace, you start to lose sight of what signals the market is sending you. Leaders can thus learn a lot from their employees if they are willing to communicate with them and understand them.

Employees want to work for an organization that is growing in a positive direction, and making that positive direction manifest is the job of the leader.

CEOs and business owners are not gods. They may be very smart, and they may be great people, but a lot of them also just happened to be in the right place at the right time so that they had an opportunity to start and own a business. I know I feel this way when I look back at my beginnings at ASG back in my twenties. I got lucky in a lot of ways, and I think ASG would have grown into an even greater success had I known early on some of the lessons that I teach business owners now.

A company will often have employees just as qualified to lead as the CEO who just haven't had the same opportunities. A leader who is willing to learn from his or her employees is one who will ultimately have a more successful company. For that reason, business owners must cultivate an appreciation for the people who work for them, and they need processes in place to enhance that over time. This includes weekly huddles, regular one-on-ones with managers, regular communication with employees. This also includes transparency, sharing things like the company financials and how the company is growing so that the company feels like one big family.

In sum, a business owner or leader must be able to communicate and be eager and willing to learn. Employees want a leader who will hear them and who will follow up on their suggestions—if the conversation is all for show, the leader will quickly lose credibility with employees.

Again, belief and engagement in a mission trumps compensation and benefits when it comes to retaining quality employees. Loyal employees are loyal because they believe in the company they work for and they want to be in a positive environment that enhances employee engagement. If you can't provide such a mission and such an environment, all the money in the world isn't going to correct it.

BUILDING A CULTURE OF ENGAGEMENT

In my last years with Ockham, we spearheaded a "Stronger Together" campaign (years before Hillary! In 2016) to try to integrate our employees more into the organization. Our focus was on fitness, since we were in the health services industry. We decided we would pick a couple of half-marathons (one in the US and one in Scotland, where our other main office was located) to run in the fall of each year, and we would start training for them in January. We gave employees extra time at lunch to run, encouraged them to raise money, and started Friday boot camps where we offered free lunch to the employees who came to train.

When time came for the race, we paid the entrance fee for any employees who wanted to participate, whether they were trying to set a world record or just go on a thirteen-mile stroll. We gave every participant a pink Ockham "Stronger Together" T-shirt and made it clear that they were all participating in the symbolic mission of the company. The first year that we did this, about 35 percent of our employees participated—which is a pretty strong representation (and also very powerful from a marketing standpoint, as I'll discuss later).

We wanted to have a direct effect; so rather than going through a large organization where we would not be able to see what our donations were contributing to, we donated the money directly to families, one in the US and one in the UK. The company matched all of the money the employees raised. We built the UK campaign around a family there that included a six-year-old girl with leukemia, whom we internally referred to as Baby Anna.

At that time, Baby Anna was going through leukemia treatment on top of being wheelchair-bound due to a chronic muscle condition. Her mom was going through a divorce, and Anna had an eight-year-old brother. We found the family due to the diligent work of some of the folks in our Scotland office. I made a trip to Scotland around the Christmas holidays, and I actually got to visit the family at the hospital where Baby Anna was being treated. I brought gifts, including an American football for the older brother. It was important to us that he not be left out, as his sister's illness and his parents' divorce were putting a great deal of strain on him too. The mom was a spectacular woman, and I spent about half an hour banging the ball around with her son (which didn't work great inside the hospital, but he enjoyed it).

I left that meeting feeling great and felt even more strongly about the mission of helping the family. The employees also were focused on Baby Anna—they knew where the money they were raising was going. It reinforced what they did in their jobs every single day. At the end of the campaign, we were able to present the family with a generous gift. Not only the recipients but also the employees were grateful that we were contributing financially to helping people. Anna has since beaten her leukemia and is managing her muscle condition well. I tell her story a lot because it is inspiring and because, when

I was at Ockham, it really solidified for the employees the idea that what they did made a difference.

AND MARKETING?

You may be wondering why I would include my discussion of marketing in a chapter that focuses on mission and employee engagement. The reason is that finding your mission and identity as a company is also a process of *branding*, and marketing is how a company displays to the world what it understands itself to be. The internal and external brands are connected—you want to present outwardly what your core mission is inwardly. If the mission of my CRO is to save lives by helping pharmaceutical and biotech firms bring treatments to market, then I want other people to know that that is our mission through our company branding.

In a sense, quality marketing only becomes possible once a company's mission is established and people are internally on board and aligned with it. How do you display your mission in a positive way? I emphasize the positive aspect because, when my company first started focusing on oncology, people would pull up our website and be confronted with pictures of tumors and serious-looking guys in white coats. People certainly knew that our focus was cancer research, but they did not leave the page thinking very positively about our business.

Our "Stronger Together" campaign, in addition to serving to strengthen company culture and employee engagement, gave us a readymade marketing tool. We could show ourselves as giving back to the community and as having employees who were passionate about our mission. Our website was now decked out with pictures of people in pink shirts smiling while they run a half-marathon, as well as the story of the "Stronger Together" campaign, pictures of healthy cancer survivors, and positive client testimonials. Now people would view the site thinking of Ockham as a quality CRO, a contributor to the community, and maybe even a cool place to work. Even if a user does not go on to do business with us or work for us, there is value in having these positive associations surrounding the brand. The Stronger Together campaign was so successful I actually received calls during the 2016 election from former employees who wanted me to sue the Clinton campaign for copying our slogan.

Quality marketing only becomes possible once a company's mission is established and people are internally on board and aligned with it.

Many business owners make the mistake of thinking that hiring a slick marketing firm is the magic bullet that will kick-start a flagging marketing campaign for them. This is not what marketing firms do. Marketing firms, at least the good ones, can help a company stream-line the marketing process and can offer advice on enhancements going forward. The business must first, however, as I have discussed, look to its financial data, especially gross margin, to discover where its value lies—in other words, identify its crown jewels and KPIs.

These feed into identifying the mission of the business, which a company has to formulate for itself before it can seek help from a marketing firm on how to implement it in its branding. If the leadership and the employees do not believe in that mission, then hiring a firm to come up with a catchy mission statement to plaster all over the walls of the office is a colossal waste of money.

I have watched more companies than I can count spend a fortune on marketing firms, assuming that a glossy new website, social media campaign, and brochures are going to get them to the promised land. If you outsource marketing, however, then what you're doing is outsourcing what you want the world to think of your business, and no firm is going to be able to deliver on this without significant input from you. So, at the end of the day, you must be invested in the marketing process, and you can't just assume that, because you're paying $10,000 a month, a marketing firm is going to do the trick for you. You have to look in the mirror at night and you have to really understand who you are, what you do, and how you do it. Once you've done that, then go use a marketing firm to broadcast that out to the rest of the country. Don't do it in reverse. Don't have the marketing firm try to tell you who you are so they can then broadcast *that* out, because it is never going to work.

All of which is to say that marketing is an all-encompassing process that only works if the company is passionate about their business and employees are willing to believe in the company mission. Marketing firms can be of assistance, but business leaders must look inward before seeking external help. The key is not a catchy slogan or a slick advertisement; the key is a sense for the mission of your business, what purpose it serves, and what makes it valuable.

> Marketing is an all-encompassing process that only works if the company is passionate about their business and employees are willing to believe in the company mission.

Finding that key to marketing can start, as I have discussed, with a sober look at the financial situation you are in, whether you are starting a new company or you are in a slump after fifteen years in business. Focusing on gross margin and KPIs means focusing on where business value lies, which means where purpose and mission can be found. Finally, that mission must be embodied in the business leader as well as lived in the company culture, through passionate and engaged employees who are aligned with the company's mission. But if you don't know where to start, just go back to that fundamental question: *Why am I doing what I am doing?*

CHAPTER 8

EVERYONE NEEDS AN
EXIT STRATEGY

I was shocked when I heard; I can only imagine how Patricia felt. She and her husband Nathan had been running a health services business for several years, with him as CEO and sole proprietor and her as his financial advisor. This arrangement fell apart suddenly when Nathan, an amateur pilot, crashed his plane into a house just outside Naperville, Illinois. He had been flying two business partners to a meeting in Chicago. All three passengers were killed in the accident, as were a young woman and a small child who lived in the house.

This tragedy affected me profoundly; I had just been meeting with him in the preceding months about potentially partnering with him and even possibly acquiring his business. My blood ran cold when I remembered his offer to fly *me* to a meeting in his private plane just a few months earlier. I had declined; I was more comfortable arranging for a commercial flight. I tried to put myself in his shoes; what was he thinking as he made his final approach, when something went terribly wrong? Was he focused on the landing, or was this just another morning commute, with his mind on the potential outcome of his meeting? Of course, it turns out that that meeting never happened, and any outcome he was hoping for is of no importance now.

Patricia was, I'm sure, personally devastated by this loss; I can't speak to her state of mind in the immediate aftermath. As I began to process it, though, it occurred to me that she and Nathan had certainly not been prepared for this type of occurrence from a business perspective, either. Nathan had no succession plan in place and had given no thought to what would happen to the business if he were no longer able to run it, even though he was nearly seventy years old. It was only by chance that his spouse, who was now owner of the business, also had a hand in running the business. Otherwise, the business would have been left with no leadership and would most likely have been liquidated.

The company's situation was much like ASG's after the death of my father. Patricia was left with a decision about what to do with the business. She ended up doing what I had done: she decided she wanted to stay committed and grow the business. Even faced with this horrible situation of their plan for their lifestyle business going awry, she embarked on a new adventure. Serving as interim CEO, she hired a new, experienced CEO after just a few months, and she went back to focusing on her strengths, which were on the finance side, as CFO.

Nathan's business had, unfortunately, been stagnating in the years before his death. His difficulty will be a familiar one if you have read the preceding chapters. He had lost focus on his crown jewel and was more interested in trying to sell a technological tool he had developed than in fostering the research services that were actually contributing to his bottom line. This technology was expensive and, worse, unfamiliar to potential clients, so they weren't buying.

Nathan didn't see this—even though the market was telling him that he should refocus on where his value lay. He had tried several times to sell the business and each time had come away offended by the offers, which he thought vastly undervalued his company. He insisted on waiting for the big score, even though he was pushing seventy and had been open to selling his business for years. He chose to ignore what the market was telling him; as a result, he was unable to achieve the kind of exit he was hoping for. Instead, his exit was a literal disaster.

Patricia, on the other hand, made the right decisions for the business—she installed a good leadership structure and refocused the business on its crown jewel, which was dermatology research. In the few years since Nathan's death, the company's value has substantially increased. Patricia is now preparing for a lucrative sale of, and exit from, the business—for even more than Nathan had been hoping for in his many years in charge.

Patricia's ability to bounce back, both personally and professionally, from Nathan's loss is admirable, and she serves as a positive example of some of the lessons I've been discussing in previous chapters. The whole scenario also really drove home, for me, the reminder that every business owner will exit from ownership in one way or another, and it is up to the owner to make that exit as beneficial as possible for the business and its employees, if it is not to be liquidated, as well as for the owner himself or herself.

EXIT IS INEVITABLE

Many owners—especially young ones, but even older ones such as Nathan—lose track of the understanding that they are one day going to exit the business world. Even if they love their work and have no plans to sell their business, no one lives forever. Those who hope to sell one day, but who have no plans to sell immediately, tend to think that the sale of the business will take care of itself at some point down the line—they will continue to grow and then get lucky and land the perfect client or make the next key innovation in their sector. Their value will explode, some eager buyer will come along, and they will cash out and live happily ever after.

This does not, however, happen automatically. Owners must work to put themselves into the position of being able to exit on their own terms and in a way that will be deemed successful in their eyes. To be in this position, they must start from where they are *now* and start making the hard decisions that need to be made to create the value that's going to enable them to have a successful exit in the future, however far down the line that may be. They do not have all the time in the world, whether they think so or not.

One way to prepare is to actually put the business on the market to see how it is valued and learn more about how your margins could be higher. A lot of owners pass on looking into selling because they are not currently planning on *actually* selling.

This is similar to an employee who has no plans of leaving his or her job; that does not mean that, if some job opening comes up, he or she should not take a look at it. However, when headhunters call people up and say, "Hey, I've got a job opening that might interest you; would you like to take a look?" about 75 percent of people say they're not looking and hang up right away. (Trust me, I know this from experience.) These people might be shooting themselves in the foot; no one knows what will happen to their current employer down the line, and if they do not know what skills to develop based on what is desirable in the job market, then they may not be marketable down the line, making it harder for them to find new jobs at competitive salaries when they *are* looking.

> Exploring the market is perhaps the most important method of determining what the value of your business is and where its crown jewels are.

Putting yourself on the job market doesn't mean committing to leaving your current job; it is just a strategy for understanding the marketplace, understanding what your value really is from the perspective of other companies and then either channeling that value into a better career at your existing company or leaving that company to go to another company with better opportunities. So why not check out the marketplace every few years? It's a smart move.

The same goes for business owners. They need to realize, "I'm going to have an exit one way or another; hopefully it will be a lucrative sale. Maybe it makes sense for me to really understand what the market might be telling me about my business now. Then I can go ahead and make changes if I need to in order for me to be in a position where my business is as valuable as possible."

Exploring the market is perhaps the most important method of determining what the value of your business is and where its crown jewels are. As a result, it is also a key way to prepare for an exit—even if you don't plan on exiting anytime soon. Neglecting to look closely at the market indicates that an owner is in denial about the inevitability of an eventual exit and about the hard decisions that must be made to prepare for it.

THE ISOLATIONIST

One way this lack of preparation for exit can play out badly for business owners can be seen in the situation of the owner I call the "Isolationist." This is the business owner who sets up a quality, revenue-generating business that works *for him or her* but structures the company in a way that prevents that value from being transferred to a new owner, thus making the company, at its current value, basically unsellable.

Let me give you an example: another husband and wife team that has been running a CRO for about twenty years. This time, however, the wife is the sole proprietor. As a result, the company registered as a female-owned business, which opens it up to being able to bid on certain government and corporate contracts that are unavailable to companies without such designation. They do some business with commercial pharmaceutical firms, but the bulk of their business—about 75 percent—is contracted through the National Institute of Health.

The business is doing well at present; however, the owner and her husband are entering their seventies and are hoping to retire soon. Their children, a son and a daughter, have taken on some of the leadership responsibilities, but neither of them envisions a long-term career with the business. Ideally, the family would sell the business, the husband and wife would retire, and the kids would go on to pursue their own chosen careers.

Unfortunately, they can't sell the company, for two reasons. First, the management structure is almost entirely built around the family members. When one company acquires another, one of the things that it acquires is the internal culture of that company, which relies heavily on management structure. Any buyer looking at this company, however, would realize that its structure and culture would simply dissolve upon acquisition. As you can imagine, this is a difficulty faced by many family businesses when they start looking into an exit strategy—many are Isolationists in this respect.

Second, another thing that a company acquires when it acquires another company is that company's book of business—that is, the customers or clients the company is currently serving. As I mentioned, 75 percent of this company's business is the fruit of its government designation as a female-owned company. Any change in the ownership structure means the potential loss of that business. No company is going to acquire another company if they know in advance that they will lose 75 percent of the other company's clients.

Because of its current structure and clientele, then, the company is basically unsellable, at least for any amount that would allow the parents to retire. If they want a successful exit, then they will need to find the ideal buyer that has the same government contract opportunities—and such buyers will be few and far between; or they will have to refocus the business away from their government work and toward their commercial clients, which would likely take years as well as massive resources to cultivate.

What is the lesson here? Well, this family has structured their business as a family business and focused on the type of work that was most convenient for them. What they have *not* done was take the time to understand the marketplace and how their company might be valued; they have *isolated* themselves from the market. As a result, their exit from the business, to be in any way successful, will first require fundamental changes to the business, which will be difficult and painful.

SUCCESSION PLAN

Another component of ensuring a healthy future for your business is putting a solid succession plan in place. I already discussed the difficulty that the lack of a succession plan caused in the case of my father's death, and a well-thought-out succession plan would also have prevented the mad scramble that occurred upon Nathan's death—though Patricia was soon able to right the ship. This, again, is a matter of business owners being aware of the fact that they will eventually exit and understanding that it may not be in the ideal way they imagine. Many owners have plans for getting millions when they sell, but not many think to put a structure in place to keep the business going if they end up no longer being able to run it themselves.

A succession plan can also help the existing owners if a business is owned by more than one person. For instance, for seventeen years I rented office space from a small office rental business owned by two older gentlemen. Fred, whom I dealt with directly as my landlord, was seventy (that seems to be the magic number), and his business partner Richard was eighty-six. One month I called Fred to renew my lease, and I was unable to reach him for a couple of weeks. Once I finally talked to him, he told me he had been recovering from a heart attack that ultimately led to heart surgery. Soon after we talked, he developed an infection as a result of complications from the surgery and soon passed away, as I learned from a tearful phone call from his assistant.

Fred and Richard, in spite of their ages and Fred's now-obvious heart condition, had made no plans for what to do with the business in case of one of their deaths. As a result, Richard, who had all but retired, became the sole proprietor. While he was still relatively healthy and in good shape cognitively, running a business was going to be difficult for him and was certainly not what he expected to be doing in those years of his life. The buildings in his care needed upkeep that he could not provide, and sadly the business's value dwindled rapidly, making a sale on his part also increasingly difficult. Again, some anticipation of these unexpected events could have helped avoid these difficulties.

When I owned my business, I had a team of high-quality legal, insurance, and accounting advisors who guided me in setting up an ownership succession plan that would provide for my wife and children in the event of my death. Thankfully, we avoided that scenario, of course; but I also felt peace of mind in knowing these things had been secured in case of a sudden tragedy. We also drew up a management succession plan so that the company would be able to continue to operate in the event of my death. I was transparent with my management team about what this plan was and the rationale behind it; they were grateful for the opportunity to provide input, as well as for the security of knowing that an untimely exit on my part would not put the company at risk.

These plans were customized to fit my business and its management and ownership structure. All of these plans should be customized, so, rather than delving into the details of these plans, I simply encourage business owners—no matter what age—to look into and seek quality advice in drafting these types of plan. This is a key component of developing the understanding that you will at some point exit the business and preparing for the best exit possible as far as is in your control.

PLAN B (AND PLAN C)

A succession plan is only the most drastic of the types of contingency plans that business owners should develop—a worst-case scenario. Backups and Plans B and C should also be constantly kept in mind. Think of it in terms of offensive strategy in football: the lucrative sale of a business at the end of one's career is the business equivalent of a touchdown. Of course, every time a team gets the ball, the coach hopes for a touchdown. At the same time, however, he has in place his special teams, waiting on the sidelines in case Plan A doesn't work out. Winning is still possible down the line if the team is prepared for all eventualities.

The business owner, likewise, must be prepared and have the foresight to know the right time to go for a field goal (the sale that may not be as lucrative as he or she hopes but will at least allow him or her to move forward) or even to cut his or her losses and punt. I suppose punting can take many forms; one example can be seen in my attempt to sell ASG in 2001.

In August 2001, a competitor came out of nowhere and offered to acquire my company for a multiple that, at the time, would have made the sale $10 million. This was a very generous offer; I was hesitant, but all of my mentors and advisors told me I would be crazy not to take it, so I ultimately agreed to it. As we were starting the negotiation process, I also began setting up a new company with a couple of partners, anticipating that it would be ready to launch in January 2002, just after the ASG sale was finalized. In the meantime, the United States suffered from the devastating terror attack of September 11, 2001. One of the side effects of this was a severe economic downturn; if our fundamentals had been strong, we would have continued to do well, but we had not been focusing adequately on our gross margin and our backlog, instead opting to keep bringing in new revenue. I soon learned that the $10 million offer was actually going to end up being $4 million.

I did not want to sell for $4 million, but my new company was almost ready to get started. I had not planned for the deal to fall through, of course, so I had to quickly readjust. I ultimately took a board seat on the second company and helped the partners hire someone to play the role I was going to play and then refocused all of my attention on building the value of ASG. This, of course, worked out well for me in the long run.

When the negotiations for the 2001 sale had started, I was expecting everything to go on without incident; however, external factors intervened and we were not well positioned to weather the downturn. As a result, I had to quickly put a contingency plan into action—namely, punting on the sale. As with football, business success is still possible in the long term if you know when to punt and are prepared to do so.

Business owners should take some time, sooner rather than later, to ask themselves some key questions; thinking about the answers will help prepare them for whatever may come moving forward.

- Do you want to sell your business for the largest dollar amount possible?

- Do you want to sell your business for less than ideal money but continue working with the buyer if the fit is comfortable and strategic?

- Do you want to sell your business and exit at close?

- Do you want to sell your business and receive some money at closing and the rest as part of a structured "earn-out" process over several years?

- Do you want to sell your business to your children or employees?

- What would you be doing if you didn't have your business anymore?

GAME PLAN

Ultimate success relies on an overall game plan, not on the assumption that a single outing is going to bring victory. Football teams do not adopt the strategy of relying on a hundred-yard kickoff return for every touchdown. Your plan for any single business—or even your business career as a whole—should not come to dominate the overall plan you have for yourself: your life plan. Business owners, even those on the verge of selling, tend to get caught up in the dollars and cents of the value of their business, losing sight of the point of it all. Even if you're about to close a very lucrative deal, have you really thought about your plan for yourself post-close?

Many will say, "I don't need a plan, I'm going to retire! I never have to work again!" But this mentality is just the problem: the plan goes beyond just your business plan or business career; you still have a life to live, and success is at stake there, too. In the final chapter, I emphasize the importance for business owners of reflecting on these larger questions. Planning your exit, your endgame for your business, should follow on, and fit into, a broader overall plan for your life.

Of course, once the life plan is in place, it will shape your exit strategy, and there are ways here and now to work toward making that exit strategy a reality. This is precisely what I have been discussing in this and previous chapters; it is also the way I understand the services I currently offer as a consultant. Rather than focusing on long-term business coaching, I offer to step in, at any point in a company's growth, and help those in charge recognize where the value of their business lies—their crown jewel—so that they can more effectively build the value of their business. I start, however, with the exit question: "What is the endgame for you?" The follow-up to that is, "How can you build your business in such a way that you will most likely achieve that endgame?"

The building of a business's value is always best approached from the point of view of a successful exit down the line—however far in the future that may be. Of course, we always have to be realistic—it doesn't necessarily make sense to hang on for that potential $20 million sale if your forecasts tell you it won't happen until you're eighty-five. In that case, the question of your broader life goals, beyond the sale, becomes very important. My strategy is to help business owners build a roadmap so they can work toward a successful exit by aligning their crown jewel and KPIs with what is valued in the marketplace. It is then up to the individual business owner to maintain the discipline to follow that plan so that he or she can have the exit that fits best with his or her overall life plan.

CHAPTER 9

THE POINT OF IT ALL

Just days after Nathan's death in a plane crash, I saw his obituary in the local paper. He was a prominent enough businessman locally that his death warranted a ten- or twelve-paragraph profile. It briefly mentioned Patricia and his children as surviving him and then launched into a chronicle of his professional and business accomplishments that read more like a resume than a tribute to someone who had passed. There was no broader discussion of family or personal life or of his role in the community. Nothing written there spoke to the *person*, as opposed to the businessperson.

I had been thinking about the rough business situation Nathan had left behind, but reading that obituary got me thinking more deeply and feeling even sadder about the situation. My thought was, "Man, that is not how I would hope to be remembered if I were to leave this earth." I have business accomplishments, of course, but I hope that there is more to my life than my work. There is more to anyone's life than what they do for a living.

This kick-started a new round of reflection for me on the matter of work/life balance. This balance had always been a high priority for me. Having lost my father when he was fairly young, I was very sensitive to the importance of making the most of the time we have with our loved ones. I was also aware of the ways in which working life can throw up obstacles to this. When I was a child, before my father started his own business, he had a job where he was obligated to travel a great deal. We also had to move many times for his work, and I can vividly remember moving trucks pulling up to the house as Dad left for work, leaving my mom home to oversee the kids as well as the whole moving process.

I don't want to overstate this: I was fortunate to have a father who never missed holidays, who was able to be home most weekends, and who was very skilled at separating work from life so that family time was made the most of; he was never distracted by work when he was with us. I also developed a strong work ethic with my dad as a role model.

I saw the downsides of his commitment to work as well, though. When I started my own career, I was of course interested in making money, but it was also important to me to have some control over my work/life balance. I was starting a family, and I wanted to make sure I could be around for my kids much more than my father had been able to be. I wanted to be able to provide for them financially and allow them to get a college education without having to take out loans, so making money was important. But I also wanted to coach them if they had any interest in sports, spend time with them on the weekends, and play a role in helping them grow into solid citizens and members of the community.

Also, even though I eventually came to own my own business, I wanted to exit from it in a way that would benefit my family without their having to join it or inherit responsibility for it in any way. I wanted them to develop their own identities and find their own ways in the business world—or wherever they chose to pursue a career.

For the most part, I had succeeded in all of these ways. However, as I read Nathan's obituary and started reflecting more, I realized that, though I had carefully arranged things so that I could be *physically* present for my family at certain times, I was not always *mentally* present. My attention might not fully be on what my kids were telling me about school; I might only give one-word answers to questions; or a phone call might pull me away from the dinner table or even from a family activity on vacation. As a result, I was not making the most of the time that I had. I decided that this needed more attention.

Work/life balance is about more than just equal time; it requires equal *attention*, which is a mind-set that is sometimes difficult for business owners to achieve. I know this simply because it was difficult for me. We get so focused on the success of our business that our success in the broader domain of life gets overshadowed. The way to avoid this is to maintain a strong sense of purpose in our work—what are the values that we work for the sake of? If we work for money, what do we want the money *for*?

Maintaining this focus is the key to a successful work/life balance. In fact, it is also central to success in the business world as well, though this may seem counterintuitive. Throughout the previous chapters I have emphasized the fact that company success is going to come from company purpose or mission; and company purpose or mission is going to be very difficult to articulate without a broader life purpose or mission.

THE PITFALLS

The reasons that this mental work/life balance is difficult are especially familiar now, due to the current state of technology. With smartphones that we carry around constantly and that allow constant access to business calls *and* email, a businessperson can be hit at any time with demands on their attention. Of course, much of the pressure this causes is self-imposed. Counteracting it, then, just takes discipline on our parts.

My friend Eric, who started and owns his own business, has one rule that he follows religiously. When he gets home from work, he places his smartphone in a basket and doesn't look at it again until he gets to work. He goes from 6:30 p.m. to 8:30 a.m. every day without looking at this phone at all.

As a CEO, Eric leads by example; he has set the tone for work/life balance at his company, and he encourages his employees to follow the same schedule he does. After all, what business-related issue is so urgent that it can't wait from late evening to the next morning? A lot of owners, being highly motivated individuals, believe they always have to be available for business concerns, as if it were a sign of weakness not to be. I can speak from experience because I used to believe this myself. I just thought it was part of contributing to the success of the business.

In fact, however, the opposite is true. Not being available 24/7 can actually empower your employees to make decisions without you, increasing accountability and a sense of responsibility in the company. Combine that with a healthy sense of work/life balance among your employees, and you end up with a fresher, happier, and more engaged workforce.

Eric is also a master of turning his business mind off when he puts that phone away. That way his attention is entirely on his family when he is with them, and the time they have together is quality time. I tried for a long time to follow a no-phone regimen such as Eric's, but my mind would continue to be on work anyway. So it is that mental aspect of it that has required a lot of work for me.

I have also been known to make the mistake of confusing quantity with quality when it comes to spending time with my family. My family makes fun of me to this day about our trip to the Magic Kingdom, where I was determined that we were going to get a turn on every ride and see every attraction in the park. When the time came to climb up to the top of the Swiss Family Robinson Treehouse, my youngest two kids were exhausted and miserable. Everything came to a head after the Main Street Parade and the fireworks—it was 10 p.m. by this time—when I was trying to drag all four kids to the log ride before the park closed. Thousands of people were streaming out of the park at the time, and I was trying to lead my family upstream. After about a hundred yards, my two youngest were crying, and my wife had had enough (as she did not hesitate to tell me). She turned around and started taking the kids to the exit, and I had no choice but to follow along.

Like I said, my kids all remember this trip, joking: "Gee, Dad, wouldn't it have been better to go to Disney World and just spend some time hanging out at the hotel pool?" My drive and motivation to accomplish had in fact gotten in the way of real quality time. I still had some work to do on turning off that business part of my brain.

UNDERSTANDING SUCCESS

Ambition drives much of the innovation in our world; I was an ambitious businessman myself, and I am proud of my success and my accomplishments. Not many of us, however, are the kind of person who will be fulfilled by sacrificing his or her family and personal life for the sake of a business. This can happen, though, if we are not careful to step back and ask ourselves about the purpose of *all* of it. For business owners, it's too easy to let business overtake our lives or to "become" what we do for a living to the degree that life takes a back seat; and this is the source of one of the most common regrets among older people who realize too late that there is more to their lives than their jobs.[2]

When we first start out, we all have a set of ambitions; we tell ourselves that once we achieve them, we will be satisfied. A twenty-five-year-old entrepreneur might write a business plan and then dive headfirst into the work required to make the objectives become realities. Once she gets there, however, it is no longer enough; she goes on to create a more ambitious plan: "I want to be a million-aire by age thirty-five," or, "I want to live in a ten-thousand square foot house." These goals, of course, take more time and energy and attention to realize; they also may overshadow the satisfaction of the achievement of the earlier conception of success.

My thought early on was, "If I can have enough money to pay for my kids' college tuition and allow us to live ordinary lives without having to make any major sacrifices, then I'll be successful. All I need is a sustaining business to make this lifestyle possible from year to year." I was able to achieve that level of success after about six years at

---

2 Rachel Gillet, "People shared their biggest regrets in life, and some of their answers will make you cry," Business Insider, accessed May 3, 2017, http://www.businessinsider.com/the-most-common-regrets-you-should-avoid/#worry-14.

ASG. I had a wonderful wife and a growing family. It was not long, though, before I had an early opportunity to sell ASG; and it hit me how much money I *could* make down the line if I were to continue growing the business.

Suddenly, I wanted more. I wanted to grow ASG into a $20 million business operating in several states around the country. That required some travel, which tipped the work/life balance a little more in the work direction. The more people I had working for me, the more attention the employees needed, which meant going in a little earlier in the morning and coming home later at night.

That's how it starts; work/life balance is compromised. The morning—getting the kids to school and yourself to work—becomes an increasingly stressful rat race. You compromise some because that's what it is going to take to get to that next level, achieve that next goal. You forget that your original goal has already been achieved. At that point, you are caught in a dangerous cycle. After a while, the whole process becomes second nature, as you continue to check off boxes and reach greater levels of success.

It is completely natural that as we and our businesses evolve, we desire greater achievement. But if we repeatedly allow one business objective to take the place of another over the course of our working lives, without attending to what we value in our broader lives, then we run the risk of missing out on important life experiences that are part of a fulfilling life. We must take the time to step back and say that enough is enough for the moment, so we can enjoy what we have accomplished so far rather than immediately moving on to the next goal. This will allow us to remind ourselves about why we started doing what we're doing in the first place: why do we have a business, why do we have families, why do we work ten hours a day? Take the time and step back to answer the "why."

I have a strong belief in *purpose* and *mission*—both in business and in life. I am also confident that no one was put on earth simply for the purpose of making money. Of course, having money is great but not if it causes you to lose sight of the things that are really valuable, such as family, church, and community. The pursuit of money should fit into, not overtake, the fulfillment of our duties to these higher values. This means we have to take care about what we devote our time and attention to.

I admire ambitious people; but I have to admit I am puzzled when I see people whose commitment is entirely to their business, though they are married and/or have children. I do see this among business owners: they are 100 percent about the business all the time, even at home. They are the busiest people on earth, but their families are ignored. At some point, though, they clearly thought that part-nering with someone in a lifelong relationship, or becoming a parent and raising a younger generation, was a worthwhile pursuit. If you want to be the best in your business at the expense of being the best husband or wife, or the best mother or father, then what was the point of entering into those other relationships in the first place?

Taking on the role of parent or spouse implies that you are willing to devote part of your life to cultivating those roles and relationships. If you have made these major life choices, then your family obligations should take priority over work; life is more, and more important than, business. Of course, the family needs financial support, and if you can contribute to that by working, then work also plays an important role in your life—but it should be for the sake of your broader life, not at the expense of it.

The businessperson who pushes himself or herself to the limit at the expense of their own physical or emotional health is also losing sight of the purpose of what he or she is doing. Neglecting self-care has negative ripple effects on one's family—and, indeed, on one's business too. I know this as a CEO who has overseen many employees: the worker who comes in and puts in an honest eight-hour day and then goes home and tends to her family, goes for a run, or gets involved in the community is ultimately more efficient, and in the long run more beneficial to the company, than the guy who is putting in twelve hours or more every day. The latter is not efficient and is not sustainable.

The constant drive to grow can also cause more problems down the line for your business. In addition to throwing off your work/life balance, it puts you at risk of compromising the success you have had so far. I made this mistake by establishing the new business unit I discussed in chapter 4. If your goal is to continue to grow, you have to be focused enough to do so without undoing the gains you have already made. This is a major part of what I help business owners with: determining and staying focused on those crown jewels and proper KPIs so that their businesses can grow without getting derailed.

This is why a business plan that fits into, rather than dominates, your life plan is so important. The life plan should come first. If your hope for your family life is to have dinner with the kids at 6:30 every single night, then fit your business schedule into that plan. If your goal is to take two weeks off every summer and go to the beach with your family, then make sure you are working with a business plan that allows that. As a business owner, as the CEO, these decisions are within your power.

I use my friend Bill as a model of the kind of successful management of work/life balance that I have been talking about. He started, owned, and ran a very successful recruiting company, while at the same time raising three successful kids with his wife. The key to his success was discipline in maintaining balance in his life. He was careful about the focus of his business, he always treated people well, and he carved out the time to become an Ironman athlete—which by itself is a triumph of discipline.

Impressively, he throws himself into everything he does with joy. When it is time to work, he is in business mode and is a great businessman. Clearly, though, given his exemplary family and his Ironman status, he focuses intensely on family and on athletic training when it is time to attend to those as well.

His business focus worked well: he achieved a lucrative exit in his early fifties. At the time, he had a strong sense of where his business fit into his overall life plan; when he saw the opportunity to sell, he knew it was a good one and he grabbed it. He started a new business but also allows himself the time to travel and to spend time with his grandchildren. He wakes up every morning with a smile on his face, ready to tackle anything life sends his way.

If you have a friend like this, who seems to just "have it all figured out," use them as a model—even as a mentor. The aim is to develop a life plan that your business plan fits into, not vice versa; and others who have done this can help you avoid some of the obstacles that will inevitably come up.

BACK TO BUSINESS

I consult with clients in their late fifties or early sixties who could easily retire from their businesses but don't because it has just overtaken their life. My advice to them is always the same: "If you want to keep working because you love what you do, then that's great; but you have to have a business plan that will fit into your *life* plan. You've only focused on the business plan; now is your opportunity to start reflecting on what role that plays in your overall life."

This goes back to how we want to be remembered and thus what our broader purpose is. No one wants to be remembered simply for making money but rather for being a good spouse, parent, or community member. For that reason, they should make those roles their highest priorities. Success will follow from that, whether in life or in business.

In fact, identifying that broader sense of purpose is a key aspect of increasing the value of a business. At Ockham, I was able to step back from gross margins and KPIs to the broader aim of the business. We didn't just bring in revenue; we supported families affected by cancer; we inspired employees to be passionate about the role they played in the oncology and clinical research world. Purpose then drives success, and the key is to focus on purpose both in life and business.

CONCLUSION

I ran track in high school, and I have always kept up with running, so I was confident that I could hold my own with this group of YMCA friends or even be faster.

I was wrong. Not long after we started running, I was trailing behind the other three. This was after the biggest of the three, Michael, had beaten me at basketball. Weeks before, during my 5:30 a.m. YMCA workout, I had seen Michael and the other two lifting weights and doing cardio, and they were clearly in fantastic shape—I couldn't lift half as much. Still, I introduced myself on the basketball court one day, and Michael invited me to join them.

Following his lead, I got stronger and faster, which of course was my aim. My attitude was that if I wanted to achieve, I should seek out someone who was achieving more than I was and get him to guide me and help me. Physical health is important to me, so I got a physical health mentor. He showed me the ropes and helped me navigate some difficulties, and his example inspired me to do better. I had thought I was doing fine until I met his crew, but it has been very rewarding to push myself beyond that status quo. This is the same reason people pay personal trainers; seeking mentors helps you do things better.

That was twenty years ago now, and we still work out together. Since then, others have joined us, and I in my turn have been fortunate to be able to serve as a mentor to others and help them become more fit.

In approaching my friend from the gym, I was just deploying an old strategy that I've used all my life and that has served me well: when I want to do something well and it is important enough to me that I am willing to work for it, I find a mentor. Mentors can help in every aspect of a person's life. Religious people seek out the leaders in their religion, or at least people who are more familiar with the religion than they might be, for advice and support; and they are right to do so. Others turn to spouses or friends—I know my wife mentors me in aspects of my life that she has mastered better than I have.

I am lucky to have mentors. I have accomplished a lot, but I didn't accomplish any of it on my own. No one does. I am also lucky to know people who do well with the kind of work/life balance I talked about in the last chapter. What all of those people have in common is that they too seek out mentors—even among their friends and family. They also often serve as mentors to other people.

The same goes in the business world. Someone who has come before you and been successful can be a source of ideas and advice— as well as warnings to not go down roads they might have. When that help comes your way, accept it. I hope that, with this book, I am able to offer some mentoring support to entrepreneurs and business owners who are trying to build their businesses and who are willing to reflect on why they are in business and what the role of their business is in their life more broadly.

The life of a businessperson is, after all, not going to be easy. The business world, like life, is unpredictable, and no one is guaranteed a free ride. Challenges will emerge, and plans will fall apart. The person who understands that, and who embraces those challenges as opportunities to start a new adventure, will be the person who will be successful going forward. Again, this is as true in life as it is in business. Businesses that overcome challenges will be stronger for it, and people who do so will be smarter. In turn, both will be able to overcome even bigger challenges down the road.

The knowledge that plans *will* go awry, coupled with the willingness to embrace those changes as opportunities, also helps you avoid one of life's most tempting pitfalls: the tendency, when things are going well, to mourn the fact that they are not going to last. I have made this mistake. Instead of enjoying the moment, I might tell myself that it is too good to be true and that something bad must be coming down the pike. This makes every great moment a little bit melancholy as well.

Michael was running a mile in just under six minutes when I started running with him. I told myself that the six-minute mile would be the goal I wanted to achieve too—and eventually I did. I celebrated this; I took a step back to appreciate what I had accomplished and take stock of it as part of my overall life plan. I could have been worrying about getting injured, or I could have let my competitive side win out and decide that six minutes wasn't actually good enough—after all, Michael was now closer to five minutes. That would have devalued my accomplishment.

I think this way of thinking is one of the biggest ways we cheat ourselves out of feeling fulfilled. This applies in business. We may have succeeded with some of our goals, but we remind ourselves that we are falling short in some other respect or convince ourselves that the other shoe is about to drop. This wrecks the moment when we should be celebrating and relishing our accomplishments.

Instead, the knowledge that life happens, or that business is business and nothing can be taken for granted, should serve as a reminder to enjoy the positive moments when they come. Then, when the negatives come—which they will—look at them not as catastrophes, but see them as potential adventures. Whatever the challenge is, you (and your business) can get through it and will be much stronger for it going forward.